Richard Harris

Actor by Accident

GUS SMITH

ROBERT HALE · LONDON

Robert Hale Limited
Clerkenwell House
Clerkenwell Green
London EC1R 0HT

British Library Cataloguing in Publication Data

Smith, Gus
Richard Harris : actor by accident
1. Acting. Harris, Richard
I. Title
792.28092

ISBN 0–7090–4133–0

Photoset in North Wales by
Derek Doyle & Associates, Mold, Clwyd.
Printed in Great Britain by
St Edmundsbury Press, Bury St Edmunds, Suffolk.
Bound by WBC Bookbinders Limited.

Contents

Illustrations

Acknowledgements

When you are faced with the rather daunting task of charting the life and career of someone whose achievements range from stage and screen stardom to writing poetry and pop songs, you rely to some extent on the co-operation of others. But when the star was also a redoubtable hellraiser the task is not made easier. In writing *Richard Harris: Actor by Accident* I was fortunate to be able to talk to his friends and colleagues in Ireland and overseas, and at the same time to draw on my own impressions as I remembered him from my days as a young journalist on the *Limerick Leader*.

My thanks to those who contributed their time and conversations during my research period for this book. Among them were stage and film directors, and a few people who, for reasons I can only respect, wish not to be identified, though their contributions were extremely important to this book.

I am particularly grateful to the following: Richard Lester, Ken Hughes, Andrew V. McLaglen, Cyril Cusack, Lise Hand, Ray McAnally, Earl Connolly, the late Colin Blakely, Fr. Tom Stack, Godfrey Quigley, Joe Kearns, Pat Billings, Tony Lennon, Eamon Gilligan, Noel Smith, Dana Wynter, Beatrice Behan, Bill Whelan, Geoff Golden, Des Hickey and Terry Keane.

Useful agencies consulted in the course of my research included the *Sunday Times*, the *Guardian*, *Sunday Express*, *Sunday Citizen*, *Hot Press*, *TV Times*, *Daily Mail*, *Mail on Sunday*, *Sunday Independent*, *Limerick Tribune*, the *Sun*, *Daily Express*, *Sunday Press*, *Sunday Mirror* and *Limerick Leader*.

Grateful acknowledgement to the following books and their authors: *Deeper into Movies* by Pauline Kael (Calder & Boyars, London); *5001 Nights at the Movies* by Pauline Kael (Elm Tree Books, London); *Hollywood, England* by Alexander Walker (Harrap, London); *Trevor Howard: The Man and His Films* by

Michael Munn (Robson Books, London); *I, In the Membership of My Days* by Richard Harris (Michael Joseph, London); *Love, Honour and Dismay* by Elizabeth Harrison (Weidenfeld & Nicolson, London); *A Paler Shade of Green* by Des Hickey and Gus Smith (Leslie Frewin, London); *The Films of Richard Lester* by Neil Sinyard (Croom Helm, London and Sydney); *Stanley Baker, Portrait of An Actor* by Anthony Storey (W.H. Allen); *The Prince: The Public and Private Life of Laurence Harvey* by Des Hickey and Gus Smith (Leslie Frewin, London); *Anthony Hopkins: Too Good to Waste* by Quentin Falk (Columbus Books, Bromley); *Peter O'Toole*, a biography by Nicholas Wapshott (New English Library, London); *Roger Moore*, a biography by Roy Moseley with Philip and Martin Masheter (New English Library, London); *What They Did in Dublin* with *The Ginger Man* by J.P. Donleavy (MacGibbon & Kee, London); *An Open Book* by John Huston (Macmillan, London); *Reed All About Me* by Oliver Reed (W.H. Allen, London); *Brando* by Charles Higham (New American Library); *The Golden Screen – Fifty Years of Films by Dilys Powell* (Pavilion Books Ltd., London); *Curtains* by Ken Tynan (Longmans); *Kirk Douglas – The Ragman's Son* by Kirk Douglas (Simon & Schuster); *No Bells on Sunday* edited by Alexander Walker (Pavilion Books Ltd., London); *Antonioni* by Ian Cameron and Robin Wood (Studio Vista, London); *The Contemporary Cinema* by Penelope Houston (Pelican, London); *Lindsay Anderson* by Elizabeth Sussex (Studio Vista, London); and *Michael Balcon Presents ... A Lifetime of Films* (Hutchinson, London).

Introduction: *A Table in the Halcyon*

The Halcyon Hotel in Holland Park, London, is small and pretty. You are likely to see there Dustin Hoffman, Jack Lemmon and Meryl Streep when they're in town.

On this leisurely spring day in 1989 the hotel's Kingfisher Restaurant was full, but at its tables were few recognizable screen stars, except Richard Harris who was dining with his ex-wife Elizabeth and an Irish journalist whose brief was to report on Harris's 'conversion'. The one-time hellraiser was no longer mentioned in the same breath as Oliver Reed. She also hoped to tell her readers whether he and Elizabeth intended to re-marry.

Harris, looking lean and gaunt, dined unperturbed. He hardly raised his voice as he reflected, 'Life is strewn with compromises and scars. In Elizabeth's and my case we need more Band-aids than most people.'

Elizabeth did not disagree. The word 'marriage' made her stop eating. 'No, we're not going to re-marry,' she said firmly. 'There's a very strong bond between us and we get on well now. Why spoil it by changing things?'

After three marriages – first to Richard, then to Rex Harrison and later to Peter Aitken – blonde Elizabeth still looked a striking woman. She had retained her superb figure and sex appeal and her vivacious personality shone through in any company. By contrast, Richard was no longer the pugnacious red-haired Irish actor of the turbulent 1960s and '70s, and the Halcyon Hotel was happy to welcome his patronage.

Today, at the table, he appeared more at ease with himself and with the world. He swore he hadn't touched the 'hard stuff' since 1981. I remember that someone had said, 'The *new* Harris is gentler, saner, teetotal and regaining his dramatic powers.'

1

Obviously it was a question of change – or else. Hypoglycaemia was diagnosed and doctors warned him that if he continued drinking he would not live more than a few months. His eating habits changed, with large amounts of unexciting oatmeal and carbohydrate to stoke him up and stop him going into shock and collapse. Obviously, this placed some restrictions on how he could enjoy himself. He admitted it was a bore, and added with a laugh, 'There must be other things in life besides drinking, though I haven't discovered what they are. Drinking is really a man's occupation. What I loved was the male camaraderie of it.'

Friends admired his courage. He fought and beat a two-bottles-of-vodka-a-day drink habit in one of the hardest battles of his life. 'I knew I had to or it would kill me,' he says. 'It was only when I crossed the line from sanity to madness that I realized it was all over.'

He liked to describe how, while playing the role of Cromwell, he saw a picture of Alec Guinness playing Charles I about to have his head cut off and told his secretary that the execution should be stopped. She immediately called a doctor, and the star decided to go 'cold turkey'.

Then he did an unprecedented thing. He filled the house with alcohol and there was vodka in every room – even the bathroom. The temptation was huge but he didn't touch a drop.

He admitted he 'dabbled in drugs'. He said he once flushed £4,000 worth of cocaine down the toilet after the drug nearly killed him. 'I had a short period when I was into drugs and I almost died,' he recalls with no hint of bravado. 'I was anointed twice. Yes, for a one month period in the mid-Seventies I used to really swallow it. I didn't know it was dangerous. Then I ended it in the intensive care in the Cedars of Lebanon.'

Now at fifty-seven, he was a resilient survivor and a realist who had no illusions any more. To his screen colleagues, it seemed a highly unusual conversion and difficult to accept, particularly his return to the Catholic Church. Harris had seen off his screen friend Richard Burton, and Peter O'Toole like himself had mellowed mainly for the same reasons – the preservation of life; only Oliver Reed seemed impervious to punishment.

In his native Limerick they found it hard to accept that Dickie Harris (they refused to call him Richard) was reformed, and a new man. In their eyes, he was untamable, his spirits – and thirst – unquenchable. 'If Dickie's off the booze, then he's not bloody well,' argued an old pal by the River Shannon. However, they had come to expect the unexpected from their folk hero and, maybe after all, he had turned over a new leaf.

They had rejected totally the notion that he could ever be a saint; that would be killing the legend they had long built up since his picturesque boyhood. There was simply no one to match him.

Now, as Richard lingered over his steamed red mullet with eel, he enthused about his latest project, Pirandello's *Henry IV*. At that moment he looked the consummate actor, playing to the gallery and providing lively companionship.

'It's the most perfect part,' he said, his blue eyes scanning the table. 'No one can resist my passion for it.' It was his sheer enthusiasm that surprised the others at the table. As ever, his enthusiasm was infectious; even the experienced woman journalist decided he was not camping it up on this occasion.

He began to retail some amusing stories, then he reflected on his film career. 'I've made forty-two films. One of them was great. *This Sporting Life*. And I've made four which were very good, *Camelot*, *The Molly Maguires*, *A Man Called Horse*, and *The Snow Goose*.'

Nonetheless, his career, as we shall see, has been decidedly chequered, complete with early triumphs, misguided choices, comebacks and disasters. He only liked to remember the good movies he had made; there were others he wanted to dismiss from his mind.

Elizabeth had by now acknowledged the change in her ex-husband. She was realist enough to recognize that certain aspects of the man would never change. She felt she understood the mercurial star better than most people. 'Dickie never left Ireland. Richard went to London.'

It was a shrewd observation on her part and she reminded the journalist at the table that she had been convinced of this for a long time. Richard grinned across the table as he remarked, 'Elizabeth's got it right this time.'

Together they were able to recollect the hellraising days in the tranquillity of middle life. Richard's wild exploits had made it hard on her. She could recall – nowadays with no hint of bitterness – when she was once cooking dinner for him in their tiny flat in London and he said he was going out for a drink. Ten days later he returned, having omitted to say the drink was in Dublin.

'I used to worry so much when that happened and would ring up the hospitals, the police stations, the airports,' she said calmly. 'But after a while I got used to it.'

As the woman journalist sipped a glass of Domaine de Lavabre, she became convinced that Richard Harris had actually changed, although the old rebel sometimes surfaced as he joked or poked fun mischievously, or fired the odd swear word into the air. She decided that 'Mr Harris was nobody's fool.'

By now they were calling him 'reclusive Harris' and the new label was not altogether an exaggeration. In his home on Paradise Island in the Bahamas he sometimes spent days writing poetry and reading, or relaxing, and thinking. He threatened more than once to write the definitive book on his own tempestuous life. Nearby on the island was his friend, the film producer Kevin McClory who had first suggested he live there.

Sober, Harris had more time on his hands. He boasted he had no need to work because of his riches, yet he retained his Hollywood agent and continued to accept film scripts. To his friends in the profession, he appeared refreshed, rehabilitated and eager for new challenges. But after two broken marriages, he showed no particular haste to marry again and continued to see a lot of Elizabeth and his children.

To some Fleet Street columnists, there was a distinct danger that the reformed Richard Harris might become a bore. The star talked endlessly about his conversion, and it did not seem to matter to him that he was repeating himself. When he talked about God and Catholicism on radio programmes there was a hint of the crusading evangelist about him. The only thing in doubt was his complete sincerity. When he was asked why he so rarely visited Limerick, he replied good-humouredly, 'Limerick is a dangerous place. Going there and not having a drink is like going into a church and not saying a prayer.'

'Dickie never left Ireland' – Elizabeth's words rang true. At any good excuse it appeared Richard popped over to Dublin from London sometimes under the guise of relaxing but more often to renew Irish friendships. Usually he stayed at the fashionable

Berkeley Court Hotel where his brother-in-law Jack Donnelly was one of the management staff.

Rumours of Richard's conversion had by now reached the Irish media and not surprisingly they were cynical, if not downright incredulous. For years they had been publishing the star's wild escapades and wondered about the truth of the claim. Was the 'big fellow' only acting? 'Irishmen don't change,' commented one *Sunday Press* columnist, 'unless they are made to.' Brendan Behan had not changed, but he was dead.

Shortly after his arrival, Harris was bombarded by telephone calls for interviews. He was determined to be selective and to the annoyance of some papers he refused interviews. He decided to talk only to certain journalists.

One of them was pop columnist Lise Hand of the *Sunday Independent*, who had done her homework on the star. 'Richard Harris is a reformed character,' she had learned. 'He has renounced drink, embraced Catholicism and lives a careful vitamin-controlled life, basing himself – when not in the Bahamas – in a small London hotel.' She decided the interview was 'going to be a piece of cake'.

That October afternoon, Harris was waiting in the hotel foyer for her. Casually dressed in a rich purple rugby shirt and canvas baggy trousers, a flowing black and white chiffon scarf coiled around his neck Isadora Duncan-style, he advanced to greet her and on recognizing the photographer with her as an old Hollywood buddy emitted a loud oath. The star then proceeded to lead his guests to the lift and up to the presidential suite on the top floor. As he perched himself on the soft couch he looked pale and wrinkled, his hair unruly, and only his eyes, alert and expressive, hinted at the Harris of more vibrant days.

Yet, Miss Hand could be forgiven for feeling nervous when he announced that 'he adored tall women', and went on to remark that giving up cigarettes had enormously increased his sex drive.

The remark, she noted from her armchair opposite, was accompanied by a speculative glance in her direction and this caused the earlier 'piece of cake' to crumble, and made her wary of his obvious charm. Secretly she told herself, 'Once a rogue always a rogue, in spite of all his protestations to the contrary.'

Looking at him, she thought he was no longer a horse of a man, yet his spare figure cut an imposing presence. And

scholarly, rounded gold-rimmed spectacles failed to conceal a
pair of piercingly bright eyes. Unable to disguise his egotism, he
bubbled with enthusiasm as he talked about the newly
established Harris Foundation in memory of his brother Dermot
who had died of a heart attack in Chicago during the tour of
Camelot. As brothers, they had been close and Dermot's death
was a cruel blow.

The Foundation would provide a scholarship for an Irish
student to study at the University of Scranton in Pennsylvania.
Richard was in Ireland to raise funds for the project.

When the phone rang, the star jumped to his feet and
answered the call instantly. Occasionally there was a knock at
the door and he rushed to open it. To Lise Hand, he was restless
and energetic, always moving about, seldom able to sit totally
still. He found time to ask her for a date, and then he suggested
dinner. She preferred to listen to his tales about his colourful
career in films.

'I remember sitting down in the dust with Richard Burton
when we were making *The Wild Geese* together,' he said
earnestly. 'We were like two old men – once the greatest
hellraisers in the world – we were too tired to stand up and pee.
After two hours of philosophical discussion, we came to the
conclusion that the tragedy of our lives was the amount of it we
don't remember, because of being drunk.'

Her notebook was almost full, but he was anxious that her
column didn't fall short and remained in full verbal flight.
Occasionally the plummy vowels of the King of Camelot slipped
into a discernible lilt. He mused, 'I've made so much money out
of so many terrible films, that the only way I can justify them is
by putting the money to good use. I've discovered there is more
to life than driving Rolls-Royces.'

He recounted with relish how 75,000 dollars changed hands
between three people on his fortieth birthday. 'Before I was
thirty, these people had placed bets that I would never reach
forty.' He took obvious delight in proving his friends wrong.
Reminiscences of his hellraising days invariably brought a
rakish smile to his lips.

Miss Hand decided she had heard enough for one day. She
politely excused herself and as she reached the door Harris
asked her for her phone number. 'He's persistent,' she thought,
and 'a charming rogue'. For her paper, she summed up:

The interview with Richard Harris had been a difficult one –
only because it is difficult to take notes when a big, strong
man keeps trying to wrestle you to the couch or insists that
you haven't seen the whole suite until you have seen the
bedroom. Maybe I should have been flattered.

Richard Harris may no longer be a wildcat, but he is
certainly no pussy cat. Perhaps the description, amiable tiger,
will do.

A week later when I talked to the millionaire star in the same
presidential suite he was restive with his feet and hands. A
compulsive talker, he seldom exercised restraint in his
utterances and quickly revealed either his likes or dislikes of
people. He confirmed that he had never any intention of taking
part in *This Is Your Life*, which to me seemed a pity for
undoubtedly his career would provide a memorable show.
Perhaps it was his lack of warmth at the time for the
programme's then presenter Eamonn Andrews, or his long-held
view that the show was too short to charter a life of real
adventure or importance.

Twice he said he had escaped the *This Is Your Life* net and he
did not hesitate to say that if Andrews had tried to present him
with the red book he would run off the stage. For a star who
loved publicity it was a curious attitude.

As he began to pace the room, he talked of his ambitions. He
wanted to star as Shylock in *The Merchant of Venice*, but soon
Dustin Hoffman would steal a march on him in that respect.
Another priority was to write a tell-all autobiography entitled
People I Did and People I Didn't. Although he refused to talk about
'borrowed time' or 'time running out' he accepted his age
without a fudge.

As he says, 'I always remember what Burt Lancaster once told
me: "There comes a time in your life when you can't get the girl
in the film any more," he said. What the group of actors of my
age – Finney, O'Toole and Burton – had was a fine madness, a
lyrical madness. We lived our lives with that madness and it was
transmitted into our work. So we were always dangerous.
Dangerous to meet in the street ... in a restaurant ... and
dangerous to see on stage or in a film.

'We had smiles on our faces and a sense that the world was

mad. *We* weren't afraid to be different. I have no regrets although I sometimes think how horrendously I behaved to some people and I feel guilty about that.'

Most people he behaved badly to tended to forgive him, attributing his obnoxious behaviour to his excessive drinking; others less forgiving blamed his personality make-up which they claimed was 'full of contradictions'. He could be generous, charming, witty and warm-hearted and on the other hand, blunt, rude and violent. A Limerick friend explained, 'Richard's innate impetuosity was aggravated by drink.'

The clown and fun-maker in Harris preferred to look back at the good times. 'Most of my excesses I enjoyed. The going was hard but it was good. I once went to see my old friend Peter O'Toole after a play to congratulate him on his performance. He looked at me over his glasses and said, "Harris, we should be dead. Think of the lives we have led – fifty lives in fifty years".'

It is Harris's millionaire status that has made the Irish take notice, as well as his success in *Camelot*. Harris is proud of his own durability as an artist and his financial independence. He has never been worried about what people think of his performances on screen; vanity is not one of his faults. Despite his lack of booze, his vitality has not diminished nor has his humour vanished. He is still reckoned good company and as gregarious as ever.

The reformed Harris inevitably attracted the attention of his colleagues; some are relieved that his hellraising days are over, others are puzzled by his conversion, a few are still incredulous.

Distinguished Irish actor Godfrey Quigley clearly recognized the change in the star. As he recalls, 'During the summer of 1989 I was playing in *A Whistle in the Dark* at the Royal Court and Dickie Harris came backstage to greet me. I had known him in the Sixties in London and knew of his wild exploits. On this occasion I found him mellowed. There was a wonderful warm truth in the man.'

Quigley listened as Harris talked about life in the Bahamas and his intention of returning to the theatre. They exchanged stories about the 'good old days' and Harris laughed in the dressing-room as Quigley recalled a few hilarious adventures.

'I could scarcely believe I was talking to the same Dickie

Harris I knew years before,' Quigley said. 'On this occasion he made a lot of sense.'

It was Harris's zest for life that he admired – and remembered. 'I think it helped him survive,' Quigley said. 'Dickie never spared himself.'

Whether he likes it or not Richard Harris is one of the immortals of show-business. This is his story.

'Dickie never left Ireland. Richard went to London.'

– ex-wife Elizabeth

1   *The birth of a legend*

'Stop that or you'll grow up like Dickie Harris' was a cautionary remark used by some irate Limerick mothers in the 1940s to troublesome boys playing in the streets. More than anything else it reflected the kind of wild reputation young Harris had acquired in the city. Later, the remark was used as a joke with no malice intended.

Harris, born on 1 October 1931 and one of eight children – six boys and two girls – was well on the way to becoming a legend. Even today, forty years later, stories abound about his remarkable exploits. Some are fictitious, others have become exaggerated with the telling, and many are true. Harris says, 'I admit to being a wild youth but if all the stories were true I think I'd want to be two hundred years of age.'

Terry Wogan was born in the same city but his early life reads like a chapter of the Bible compared with the Dickie Harris saga. Like Wogan, young Harris went to Crescent College and was taught by the Jesuits. Soon he became a character in school, was fond of clowning and was more gregarious than most of the other students. He lacked academic ambition and instead concentrated on rugby football in which he excelled as a forward. In the late 1940s he was a member of the college's winning cup teams, and his outgoing personality and sense of fun made him popular with his teammates.

'Members of the rugby team were given extra privileges and special treatment,' he recalls. 'This suited me fine because I was never academically very bright.' Once when a teacher came round to his desk to distribute term examination papers he just looked at them and proceeded to build paper houses out of them. Then he put his head down and fell asleep.

Although he was somewhat overshadowed by his brother Noel as a stage performer, young Dickie, tall and broad-shouldered, was cast in the school plays and musicals. He possessed a reasonably good singing voice, which was light in timbre, and his performance in the William Vincent Wallace opera *Maritana* won praise from his teachers.

It was noticeable though that he acted up to his wild image and soon became a hero with many of his friends. 'He was always up to some mischief,' said one of his classmates. 'But we liked Dickie a lot.'

He never worked hard at his school work. His father, Ivan Harris, who had been educated at Downside in England, would say resignedly, 'Let the boy go his way.' When he didn't turn up for school he imagined that the Jesuits were actually pleased. 'I think they considered that I lowered the standards of the school.'

The Harris boys, Dickie, Jimmy, Ivan, Noel and Billy, shone at rugby and tennis; their brother Dermot did not participate in sport to any great extent. Dickie's ambition from an early age was to be a top rugby footballer and wear the green jersey of Ireland. It was accepted that he would never make a scholar.

While Crescent College turned out students who would become lawyers, doctors and bankers, it also put much emphasis on sport and over the years a number of its former pupils played rugby for Ireland. The Jesuits maintained a tight discipline and students who caused trouble or neglected their homework were punished. The punishments, which were carried out by the College Prefect of Studies, ranged from two slaps, or biffs as they were called, on the hand, to six slaps, depending on the gravity of the offence. The prefect used a leather strap and this became a dark symbol in itself. Boys came to fear the strap, but young Dickie Harris shrugged it off as something to be endured like a hard rugby tackle on the field.

The Harris family was close-knit and resided in a large house known in the area as Overdale. It was full of vitality and its doors were always open to the children's pals. For young Dickie it was a particularly happy and vigorous childhood. His father's flour mill provided the money to ensure that the family lived a life of quality. Young Harris was born into a conservative, class-conscious Limerick where the madcap antics of wealthy young men were accepted with stoic understanding by the barmen and hotel porters of the city.

It was a city, small and compact, that was emerging from the deprivation of a world war, with attitudes firmly rooted in faith and morals. Any display of new thinking or challenge to the established order was frowned upon. Harris and his youthful pals were the first generation to break away from values inculcated down the decades. They represented a more open and liberal approach, a foretaste of the new generation whose confidence and social standing were dictated by family tradition.

He was a young rebel, always the centre of fun and mischief, admired by youth, regarded with some intolerance by an older generation. 'Dickie's incorrigible' was a phrase often used about him, but he ignored public opinion. In the streets he was conspicuous by his flaming red hair, gangling figure, and loud, musical voice. He could be quick and devastating with his tongue. Pretty girls – and Limerick had more than its share – tagged along after him and sometimes joined in his mischief-making and pranks, though it was generally accepted that he preferred at that time the company of boys of his own age.

Cinema-going was a popular pastime in the city and as long as he can remember Dickie Harris loved movies. They fired his lively imagination, fed his fantasies, and created for him new heroes. He was able to run off the names of screen cowboys and gangsters with admirable speed. 'One of my most abiding memories of Dickie,' recalls a schoolboy friend, 'was of seeing him falling down the wide staircase in the Savoy Cinema as he imitated the contortions of the cowboy star he had just seen in the cinema. He was very good at that. We used to be entertained to his rather robust gymnastics and he liked to show off.'

It was ironical, therefore, though no great surprise to some of his pals, that he was banned at different times from all the city's cinemas. 'I often went to the cinema and stayed there all day,' he recalls. 'I would go in for the matinee, stay for the middle show and evening performance. I used to do that when I had nothing else to do, especially in the summertime when I was on holidays. Later on when I started drinking I would go into the cinema drunk and I would stand up, sometimes on my seat, and start to say the lines with the actors.

'There is a famous story about the time I got drunk and went into the Lyric Cinema where Marlon Brando was playing in *Julius Caesar*. When I got there I proceeded to repeat the immortal lines, "Friends, Romans, Countrymen, lend me your ears." Then I went on, "I have not come to praise Caesar but to bury him," which immediately made the audience laugh. Well, a Garda squad car pulled up outside and I was taken away for causing a disturbance.'

It was not long before he was recognized by cinema doormen and stopped. But life continued to be fun. His first love was a girl called Grace Lloyd, but he was to say sadly, 'We grew up together but she had no love for me. Grace was always the "humdinger" in my life, the girl I cared most about.'

He was not unaware of the fact that he was growing up in a fairly privileged family, whose lifestyle contrasted with the poverty and poor housing conditions not a mile away from his home. The Harrises were among the lucky families at that time, for they were never short of food at Overdale. They kept a nanny, a servant and a gardener, and there seemed to be plenty of money for the good things of life. Gradually however, the flour-milling business began to decline, which meant that one or two of the house staff had to be let go.

'When this happened I realized change was coming,' he recalls, 'and the full realization struck me when my mother began to do the washing.' It was an exaggeration, however, to claim that the family fell, as Harris occasionally says today, on 'poor times'. It never came to that.

He admits he did a lot of foolish things as a youth, yet he invariably takes intense pleasure in recalling those childhood days in Limerick. 'I remember going to Cruise's Hotel every Saturday night at nine o'clock to wash dishes. My payment was free entry to the dance, and that was the highlight of the week, my big night out.

'Between dances, rugby and music I was kept going twenty-four hours a day. Myself and my pals, Gerry Murphy and Paddy Lloyd, would go out together a lot. When we went to the pictures only one of us paid to get inside and the other two would go round to the fire exit. When one of us was inside then he would go to the fire escape and duck the other two in. This worked at the Savoy, Lyric and the Carlton, but it was difficult at the City Theatre and the Grand Central.'

In Kilkee, the popular County Clare seaside resort more than sixty miles from Limerick, he became known as the 'lively lad'. In summer half the population of Limerick repaired there for holidays. It became known colloquially as Limerick sur-mer. Harris's red hair and long, lean body could be easily picked out on the expansive beach, or when he played volley ball against the whitewashed wall at the sea-front.

In the local Arcadia Cinema he was among the Limerick lads who shouted remarks at the screen and each other, or chanted along with the ads. The cinema bill changed nightly. Occasionally Harris's voice could be heard above the din and the usher would shout, 'Silence!' Sometimes the audience chorused along with a popular ad of the time to the tune of Danny Kaye's 'Wonderful Wonderful Copenhagen':

Wonderful wonderful golden
Amber ...
A beautiful flavoured tea
When you drink a cup
It will cheer you up
Wonderful golden
Aaaammmbbberrr.

When he left Crescent College his father suggested that he go into the flour-milling business. 'There was not much else I could do,' says Dickie. He became popular with the customers as he sold flour over the counter and in a jokey voice would count out aloud their exact change. The old ladies enjoyed his easy manner and sense of humour. As flour millers they had big barns and lofts and sometimes the wiry young Harris spent his time frightening the mice away from the flour.

His ambition to be an international rugby player was still a top priority with him. He had wanted to play for Young Munster but his father persuaded him to join the famed Garryowen club, and in 1952 he won a Munster Senior Cup medal with Garryowen. Good rugby judges considered he had a promising career provided he concentrated on the game. However, he still found time to play pranks. Once his father insisted that he attend a special tennis tournament being held at the local county tennis club where the Harris family were founder members. It was reckoned an important competition. The West of Ireland Championships always attracted a big entry of talented players.

On arrival at the club with his pal young Harris's attention was instantly drawn to the giant winners' cup surrounded by plaques, medals and trophies placed on a table near the gents' toilet. He also realized that a fellow could easily open a small window at the rear of the toilet and remove the cup.

'So without further thought, I quietly entered the toilet,' he recalls, 'went to the window, opened it, leaned out and removed the cup. I then placed it in the boot of the car and waited to see what would happen. It took a little while for anyone to notice but eventually there was consternation and havoc when word got out that the cup had gone missing.'

The finger of suspicion almost immediately was pointed in his direction. As he says today, 'It was generally believed that Harris was responsible for nicking the cup but nobody dared challenge me on it and when I left the grounds afterwards there were no questions asked.'

The newspapers published the story. Harris hid the cup in an unused corner of his home and thought no more about it, although he had intended returning the cup in a few days. The next morning when he arrived home he was confronted by his father.

'Jesus, Mary and Joseph, Dickie, get that cup out of this house,' he ordered his son. Ruffled, Dickie tried to explain away the prank but his father would not hear of it, repeating instead the words, 'Get the cup out of here.'

He went to Cruise's Hotel where his brother-in-law Jack Donnelly was the general manager, and quietly went to the ladies' toilets, the cup under his arm, and locked himself into one of the cubicles. He placed the cup on top of the toilet seat, then unlocked the door and hurried through a corridor to the rear of the hotel, where he hopped over a wall. He then went in to a public phone and rang the Garda station and told them where the cup could be found. Within minutes a Garda squad car arrived outside the hotel and four officers ran inside and, in a few moments, emerged with the cup.

Later, the cup was presented to the tennis tournament winner by politician Donogh O'Malley and when he heard who was suspected of taking it in the first place, commented 'I wouldn't put it past the blackguard.'

In 1952, just when it appeared that his rugby career was taking off with Garryowen, Harris was stricken with tuberculosis but his mother would not allow him to be sent to a sanatorium; instead she decided to nurse him at home in Overdale. At the time in Ireland the disease was rampant and there was a certain stigma attached to anyone going to a 'San'. It took young Harris weeks, perhaps months, to accept that he would be confined to the house. For a restive and athletic young man it was sheer agony.

During the long, tedious days and nights he began to read and think a lot. Gradually he came to terms with himself and at the same time discovered who his real friends were.

'At first people came to see me every day, then after a while they got bored with me just lying there so they left me alone and I continued to develop my imagination; light bulbs, doorknobs, pillows became animated objects and I began playing scenes with them as if they were real people. I also read a lot – letters of Van Gogh in particular, and they turned me on to a kind of self-search that has never stopped.'

In the room, as he lay propped up in bed, he recited lines from plays aloud, especially Shakespeare and soon he was able to close the book and recite whole passages. He imagined himself on stage playing Hamlet or Romeo and the thought made him want to get better quickly. 'I want to be an actor,' he told himself as the sunshine lit up the room. 'But how am I going to go about it?'

When he was finally told he was clear of TB, he announced his decision to become an actor to the whole Harris household. He also convinced others that he was deadly serious. One day in O'Connell Street he met a former school friend, Tom Stack, who was then studying to be a priest. They talked about little else except acting.

'I remember Dickie had a copy of John Steinbeck's *East of Eden* under his arm and this was a revelation to me because I remembered that at school he showed little interest in literature. When he told me what he was reading I was fascinated and knew he wanted to be an actor. I could see, despite his illness, that he had lost none of his humour and zest for living.'

Although Harris had seen McMaster and MacLiammoir and Siobhan McKenna when they visited Limerick, he claimed it wasn't their influence that made him become an actor. His motivation came from his reading. He conceded however that he learned a lot about acting from professional touring companies. 'I remember the Lord Longford Group came to Limerick with their production of Pirandello's *Henry IV* and I was staggered by the play. I swore that one day I would play the lead.'

He began to take an interest in local amateur drama companies like the College Players. As his interest grew, he thought of going to live in Dublin and applying to the Abbey Theatre for work but he dismissed the thought from his mind: he knew nobody in the theatre there and doubted that he would get a job. His mind was made up for him when the Anew McMaster company visited Limerick. 'If you want to be an actor, my boy, you must go to London,' McMaster advised him.

Around 1954, a combined university drama group arrived at Kilkee to present plays. Harris got friendly with them and agreed to cook their meals in the big house overlooking the sea called Hatter's Castle. At night he helped backstage with props and scenery. It was the first time he had worked with a drama group and he enjoyed the experience enormously.

On summer nights the hotels held singalongs and the entertainment proved very popular with visitors. Everyone was expected to do their party piece. One Sunday evening in the Victoria Hotel, a very popular venue, Harris was drinking with his Limerick friends and listening to a singer belting out a big ballad to piano accompaniment when a voice was heard exclaim, 'Give us Brando, Dickie.'

When the singing stopped, the request was repeated. Everyone knew it was Harris's favourite party piece and they never tired of asking for it. It was a lengthy sequence from the movie *On the Waterfront*, featuring Marlon Brando. Harris stepped forward and took the centre of the floor. Silence fell in the large room.

Using an American accent, and in a hushed voice he began to 'take off' Brando convincingly. 'There was a touch of the method-acting school about his performance,' recalls Tom Stack. 'His gestures, whispered words like "I coulda been somebody, instead of a bum ..." caught the flavour of the movie to perfection. The audience was captivated.'

To Stack at that time, Harris was a great extrovert and possessed both personality and presence. They talked together again about the vocation of acting and he felt that Harris was then more determined than ever to pursue his chosen career. 'It was eating him up and I could see he would never be satisfied until he was an actor.'

It was clear, too, that Limerick was becoming too small for him. He was misunderstood by many of its citizens who confused his Bohemian ways with lack of purpose and talent. Once when the veteran editor of the *Limerick Leader*, Con Cregan, met him on the stairs of the building, he nodded his head and told a member of his staff, 'I met that eccentric young Harris on the stairs just now. What ever is to become of him?'

Joe Mulqueen, the stocky middle-aged chief reporter drew on his pipe and replied, 'They say he wants to act.'

Cregan shook his head, and said, 'My God, that young man has been play-acting all his life. And he's such a sturdy fellow, you know. Couldn't he do something useful with himself?'

Harris knew he had to get out of a city that thought more of shopkeepers than of actors. For an aspiring actor, there were few opportunities to learn the techniques of the art of acting. When he told his father he was leaving the mill job, he wished him well but he was not surprised by his son's decision.

Harris was able to look back on a happy time in Limerick. As he says, 'I had a great childhood, and I don't regret a single day of it. Limerick was good to me. Sure I had troubled and happy times but all in all, I love the place.'

'Dickie was as wild as he was painted,' mused Limerick show-business columnist Earl Connolly. 'But it was only mischief and a bit of devilment; I don't remember him ever being vicious or nasty. I knew he wanted to go on the stage but I wasn't sure about the extent of his talent and had no idea how far he would go.'

Michael English, whose mother had a deep interest in theatre, knew of Harris's ambition to be an actor. They were friends and Harris confided in him his hopes for the future. 'My mother once made Dickie and myself go on stage with Anew McMaster when he visited Limerick with his company. He was proud of that. Dickie knew what he wanted.'

One of Harris's best pals at that time was the aspiring poet Desmond O'Grady who remembers Limerick as 'a caste-divided city of Catholics and Protestants, urbanites and suburbanites, Laurel Hill and Presentation girls, Jesuit and Christian Brother boys. The rugby, rowing and church clubs were equally divided.'

To O'Grady, the arts were very local and low key but there was himself seriously writing poems and Dickie Harris dedicated to becoming an actor. They both had their personal epiphanies; through his lonely reading Harris discovered plays and books and O'Grady discovered poetry.

'During this hiatus of adolescence,' recalled O'Grady, 'Harris realized the radiance of Marlon Brando and the modern New York School of method acting. I discovered James Joyce and the modern movement in literature. Our painter friend Jack Donovan discovered Cézanne and modern painting. We three became fast friends.'

They met frequently in the Savoy tea-rooms to talk endlessly about the arts and their own particular ambitions. Because they had little money they were grateful to the 'innocent waitress' who grew to like their presence there and kept their teapot refilled with hot water. Sometimes they even imagined they were in some famous café in London or Paris, aspiring artists discussing their future work.

At other times, they went along to the Carlton Cinema to see the early Brando films and any forbidden Continental movies. They dressed in 'arty clothes', with young Harris prominent in his newly fashionable duffle coat and O'Grady looking like James Joyce in his clerical blackcoat and sweater. The painter Donovan wore crumpled country clothes and a battered tweed hat.

Being different from most others of their age in Limerick, they were labelled 'eccentrics'. O'Grady had made up his mind to try his luck in Paris, Harris talked about art schools in London, and Jack Donovan was content to go on painting wherever he could. With a poet's imagination, Desmond O'Grady was particularly anxious to leave the narrow confines of a city which he described then as 'the last bollard on the dark edge of Europe, and O'Connell Street seemed a Desolation Row for anybody with a curious imagination'. Young Dickie Harris did not see Limerick in such black shades, nor did he wish to. Perhaps it was because of his abiding love for rugby football and his favourite teams, Garryowen and Young Munster.

His previous confinement through illness had had the effect of tending to make Harris more introspective on occasions, though it was never for long. Soon the old impetuosity would surface as well as his unquenchable humour and penchant for clowning. But if some Limerick people believed that there was little more to him than a mere prankster, they were wrong. He was ambitious, determined, and had a specific goal. Yet certain facets of life puzzled him. He sometimes wondered, for instance, what mark he had made on his parents; he was closer to his mother than his father.

'There were six boys and two girls in the family,' he likes to recall, 'and I was lost in the middle of this Harris brigade. I was the non-commissioned officer in the middle! I can't remember the parental stroke, the touch from mother or affection from father, that sense of being singled out, so I had an identity crisis when the tuberculosis eased off. I was free to become something, but what?

'I chose acting partly because I knew I'd have to create an identity for them to recognize I wasn't just child number five. I wanted them to realize who I am, for my mother and father to say, "Hey, we've got a friend called Richard Harris in the family. That's him there on the stage." '

He has always spoken of Limerick with passion and a tinge of sadness. His memories are vivid and mostly happy. He once recalled his earliest memory:

'My brother Noel was just born and one day I was pushing him in the pram. My mother and the maid were behind us and we were walking down Post Office Lane and the maid said, "Richard, whatever you do, do not take your hands off the pram." Then, for some reason, I looked into the pram and saw Noel and asked my mother would I ever be that young again? She leaned over to me and said, "No, Richard, you won't." '

Harris has always been able to tell a joke against himself. Once, he recalled, 'I remember well an American journalist who went to Limerick some time ago to do a story on me. She knocked at the school door and asked to speak to the Head. When he came down she asked did Dickie Harris go to school here? and explained that she was doing an article for an American magazine. He said, "I'd prefer you did not mention him in relation to this school." '

If the Jesuits at Crescent College failed to make an abiding impression on Harris, at least he carried away with him a love of rugby football and the meaning of friendship, for over the years he has retained an interest in rugby and kept friendly with former classmates. Now, in 1955, at the age of twenty-four, he was preparing to start a new career in London.

Being an extrovert the city would scarcely overwhelm him. Some people in Limerick heaved a sigh of relief when the news broke that he was leaving; others continued to retail funny stories about his zany escapades, and a few wondered if he would ever make it as an actor.

Dickie Harris was determined to prove everyone wrong.

2 'Academy is right up my street'

In London he went for an audition to Central School. It was an experience he was unlikely to forget.

'I walked in with all these aristocratic-looking ladies and gentlemen sitting there, looking at me, saying, "What are you going to do for us, young man?" So I said Shakespeare. I did my piece and afterwards they said to me, "What right do you think you have to enter our profession?" So I looked up and said, "The same right as you have judging me." Then a bell rang, and a little man came in and they put me out.'

The main reason he believed he was turned down was that he was a little ugly, and it wasn't the day of the ugly young man, but the day of the John Nevilles. Today, he says with a shrug, 'When it came down to brass tacks, I suppose I wasn't good enough.'

He wanted to be an actor and rejection didn't mean the end of the world for him. He almost immediately applied to the London Academy of Music and Dramatic Art and to his surprise was called for audition. He performed a bit of *Richard III*, a bit of *Cyrano de Bergerac* and some improvisations. They told him he had been accepted.

At twenty-four he was the oldest student there; the ages of the other students were around seventeen and eighteen. He buckled down to study as best he could, but on his own admission he wasn't a very good student. 'Probably because I was older,' he said, 'I twigged after a short time that academies are geared for stage management, make-up, carpentry, wardrobe. I decided that if I were to fail as an actor I wasn't going to become a stage manager or a carpenter.'

He was in luck. LAMDA was the only academy in London with a Stanislavsky class, and that was the class he most wanted to join. Method acting appealed to him, and in this respect

Brando was his hero. It suited his uninhibited style and temperament, and in any case he wasn't interested in any other kind of acting at the time. He reckoned the classical theatre could wait. Fortunately, he found that he excelled in the Stanislavsky approach. At the same time he was also keen to direct, but there were no classes for directors in London.

However, he soon found himself directing the end-of-term shows: scenes from Shaw's *Saint Joan* and Miller's *Death of a Salesman* – and *The Playboy of the Western World*, which he managed to condense into a one-acter.

He was no longer Dickie Harris. The students called him Richard and he had no complaints. Outside the academy, he drank in pubs, stayed up late, and met Irish actors seeking work. He was satisfied with his own progress, though money was scarce.

It was a stimulating time to be joining the London theatre scene. New playwrights were emerging, and already Joan Littlewood's Theatre Workshop was making its mark at Stratford East. He made the rounds of the theatres and was able to see Beckett's *avant-garde* play, *Waiting for Godot* at the Arts, directed by Peter Hall, and Paul Schofield's *Hamlet* at the Phoenix. The play attracted him greatly and one day he hoped to tackle the title role. He began to interest himself in what the critics, Ken Tynan and Harold Hobson, had to say. Tynan, in particular, he found acerbic and entertaining. He knew he was regarded as the most influential critic on the London theatre circuit.

Harris by now was a young man in a hurry. He was prepared to make any sacrifice to achieve his goal. Endless opportunities in the theatre, TV and films were there to be grasped but first he knew he must learn the actor's craft. It did not depress him to find scores of young men like himself seeking fame and fortune, though he increasingly wondered how eventually the 'breaks' would come his way.

One day he had an unexpected visitor to his dingy bedsitter, the poet Desmond O'Grady who was barely eking out a living in Paris. Seeing his old Limerick 'arty pal' cheered up Harris no end; they hadn't met since they had gone their separate ways a year before.

'Two almost penniless Paddies in a London winter cut a pitiful picture,' recalls O'Grady. 'We talked about what we were doing, plays and poems. And we talked about *Finnegan's Wake*. Even fought over it.'

Later that evening they visited a local fish and chipper. With such little money they could only afford one serving which they shared. Again the waitress, as in the Limerick Savoy, liked them and served them extra large helpings. To Harris, the young poet was great company, tense, knowledgeable and sincere. He promised to visit him in Paris when he could afford such a luxury.

Suddenly, luck turned his way. On another evening he was drinking in a pub with O'Grady, and feeling a little desperate, when they heard somebody in the next alcove saying that Joan Littlewood was casting for a new production of Brendan Behan's play, *The Quare Fellow*, at the Theatre Workshop. Harris looked at O'Grady, and said, 'Christ, I'll have a try for a part in that.' He borrowed some change and telephoned the Workshop and spoke to Gerry Raffles, the manager, and asked him if he could come for an audition. Raffles said there was only one part available.

'How old are you?' he asked Harris.

When he told him he was twenty-five, he said, 'The part is for a fifty-year-old.'

Harris sounded desperate.

'I promise you I look fifty. I haven't eaten for months or slept for weeks. Christ, don't turn me down. Let me come and see you.'

Raffles must have been impressed by Harris's sheer persistency, for he replied, 'If you want to come out, I'll see you.'

Harris returned to the pub and borrowed more money from O'Grady and took a tube to Stratford East. Half-way through the audition, for which he used the improvisation on which he had worked hard at the academy, Joan Littlewood stopped him.

'Look,' she said rather impatiently, 'you're far too young for the part. But there is another part, the part of Mickser, and I'm not too happy with the casting. Would you like to play it for ten pounds a week?'

Harris, on his own admission, nearly collapsed with delight and fright. He would be able to eat – and sleep – in a little more comfort in the weeks ahead. An aunt of his had left him some shares in Guinness and these had put him through the academy. When he had paid his fees he had only two pounds a week with which to pay for a room and food.

What thrilled him more than anything else, however, was meeting Miss Littlewood; he felt he had known her for years. Their temperaments did not clash and he looked forward tremendously to working with her. Theatre Workshop, he felt, was *his* scene, where he could use some of the Stanislavsky training he was acquiring at the academy.

Although their meeting had been brief, he was certain he could learn a lot about acting from her and, if lucky enough, be invited to be part of the company. The prospect excited him.

Attending RADA at this time was a pretty Welsh blonde, Elizabeth Rees-Williams. Ever since she had played Sir Peter Teazle in *School for Scandal* at college she had been eager to be an actress. But now, in her fifth term at the academy, she wasn't at all sure whether she would ever attain star status. Her confidence was further eroded when the academy Head, John Fernald, told her that in his opinion her future as an actress was 'limited'. Self-doubts assailed her, and she began to question her own dedication and discipline.

Furthermore, her background did not equip her ideally for the onerous profession. She had spent a year in a convent in Switzerland and now there appeared to be so much lost time to make up, so many parties to attend, so many young eligible young men to meet. Distractions everywhere. It became a question of time, for late nights left her somewhat jaded for drama classes, although she denied this was the case.

Her philosophy was summed up in her own words at the time, 'Sleeping seemed such a waste of time. I firmly believed that the quality of one's life was shaped by cheerful insomnia and an unyielding sense of pleasure. I was blessed with both. Nothing, I felt, was too strenuous for my constitution.'

She had fallen in love on several occasions, but 'always for a span too short to be painful'. From time to time her parents, Lord and Lady Ogmore, worried about her hectic lifestyle in London and her progress at RADA. They wondered if she could combine the two successfully.

At this time she heard from a casual friend, the actor Peter Prowse, that they were casting the Clifford Odets play, *Winter*

Journey and there might be a part for her. It was to be a West End production and would be directed by a newcomer, Richard Harris who, it was rumoured, had invested his savings in the play.

Together they arrived at the Troubadour coffee bar, which was cosy and dimly lit. The place had a good name in the business and its owners, Sheila and Michael Van Bloeman, assisted 'resting' actors, homeless musicians and aspiring artists. In the crowded and smoky interior there was a faint sound of guitar music, but in the candlelight it was difficult to pick out faces.

Elizabeth followed Prowse to a table where a man was sitting alone. As they took their seats, he slowly lifted his head from the book he was reading. Suddenly, Elizabeth felt nervous. She heard Peter Prowse say, 'This is Richard Harris.'

She introduced herself as Elizabeth Rees-Williams and his unsmiling response made her feel uncomfortable. He rose and towered over them. He asked Prowse to accompany him downstairs to the cellar, and after some time she was summoned there. Harris handed her a script and asked her to read the part of the young girl. In the unusual atmosphere she was uncertain how she sounded and Harris gave no hint of what he thought. A week later she was told she had got the part.

Winter Journey was scheduled to go on at the tiny Irving Theatre off Leicester Square and it was already doubtful whether Harris would recoup his investment in the production. During rehearsals, Elizabeth continued to live it up at night and took cocktail parties in her stride. Harris at first was unaware of such distractions in her life, though he could not help noticing that she was dropped off for rehearsal in a posh car. As director he was far too engrossed in the play to pursue the matter.

Lord Ogmore took an interest in the play and intimated that he would attend the first night. According to an interview Elizabeth Harris gave to *Women's Own*, it was noticeable that during the performance Harris 'paced up and down the narrow aisle in the auditorium; he punctuated the actors' speeches with sharp intakes of breath, and uttered curses so audible that heads swivelled in his direction.'

Lord Ogmore was to note that Harris went about with his shirt hanging out of the seat of his trousers; for the peer it was a novel and rather startling experience.

Although they had known each other for six weeks, Elizabeth could see that Richard had shown little or no interest in her private life, yet when he was told later by members of the cast that she was a deb, he was furious, and announced, 'The first time she's so much as two minutes late for rehearsal, she's out on her social ass.'

They did not seem attracted to each other. 'We seemed, on the face of it, utterly incompatible,' she recalls. 'I suppose more than anything else, I was afraid that he would despise me and my way of life, my background and friends.'

It struck her that he could be antagonistic, rash and quick-tempered. But she found his Irish brogue attractive and his vitality astonishing. He frankly admitted that he had backed a loser in *Winter Journey* but, being an eternal optimist, hoped for better luck next time. Elizabeth overlooked his impulsiveness, yet she was not always prepared to let him off lightly. In verbal combat, she gave as good as she got. Richard, she decided, respected a fighter. And he had shown enough personal ambition, and theatrical involvement, to reassure her that he was serious about the future.

So she did not hesitate to accept an invitation to visit his cousins in the English countryside. She found it 'irresistible'. As he talked about famous Irish writers, she listened engrossed; he was strikingly different to the young men she had flirted with as a débutante. Inevitably they became lovers. 'I simply wanted to be near him,' she said. Despite their different worlds, she was now emotionally and sexually attracted to him; he was a romantic and made her feel a risk-taker. For him life was an adventure.

She let her parents into the secret. At first, they were puzzled and uncertain of what to think. They had heard of the insecurity of the acting profession and were worried. Elizabeth persuaded her mother to invite Richard to dinner and though she had an air of 'worried remoteness' about her at the table, the occasion was enjoyable and, as Elizabeth said, 'worth the risk'.

With his solid social background in Limerick, Richard could hardly be called a 'working-class actor', though working at Theatre Workshop identified with that *genre*. Nor did he feel an outsider in upper-class society, indeed he spoke to Lord Ogmore on equal terms. He explained his financial circum-stances with typical frankness and showed no particular embarrassment when asked, 'Are you trying to say you wish to marry my daughter, young man?'

Harris simply replied, 'Yes, I am.'

Eventually the peer gave his permission, despite Lady Ogmore's serious reservations. She was concerned about her daughter's future and would probably have preferred an army colonel as a son-in-law instead of an impoverished young actor – and an Irishman to boot.

The news of their engagement in the spring of 1956 was noted by the social columnists of Fleet Street. In Limerick they said it was an extra string to his bow. Once again Dickie Harris had done the unexpected and got engaged to a peer's daughter. The *Limerick Leader* published the news and for weeks it was a topic of conversation in the pubs and hotels.

There was a look of surprise on the face of the *Leader*'s editor, Con Cregan, as he read the story in his own newspaper. Turning to his chief reporter, Joe Mulqueen, he said, 'That young Harris is going places. Is it true she's Lord Ogmore's daughter?'

Mulqueen smiled. 'I hope so. That's what we say in the *Leader* anyway.'

What both men didn't know was that Harris was planning to introduce his bride-to-be to Limerick's puzzled citizens.

Brendan Behan's *The Quare Fellow* opened on the evening of 24 May 1956. Theatre Workshop was packed for the occasion. Everyone, including Joan Littlewood and Harris, who was playing Mickser, suspected that the rumbustious Behan was determined to steal the limelight. In a raucous voice he intoned the opening song, 'The Old Triangle'.

> A hungry feeling came o'er me stealing
> And the mice were squealing in my prison cell.
> And that old triangle
> Went jingle jangle
> Along the banks of the Royal Canal.

While Richard Harris was no Dublin-born republican, he understood the playwright's rebel sympathies and regarded him as a writer of wit and passion. In his view, he had drawn authentic prison characters in *The Quare Fellow*, skilfully capturing the language and behaviour of the inmates, and it was a powerful statement against capital punishment.

As an individual, he found Behan lively company, irreverent and anti-establishment. At the final curtain, the playwright, noisy and in an open shirt collar, jumped on to the stage and made a speech to the audience, then sang 'The Old Triangle' again. His reputation had preceded him to London and the press was there in force. Harris and the cast did not begrudge Behan the limelight.

The importance of the play, which had an all-male cast, was reflected in the reviews. *The Times* described it as 'a powerful portrait of life in prison', and W.A. Darlington in the *Daily Telegraph* called it 'an unusual evening'.

When Harris read Kenneth Tynan's eagerly awaited verdict in the *Observer* he agreed that the critic had 'hit the nail on the head'. Tynan hailed *The Quare Fellow* as Brendan Behan's tremendous new play, and added 'Joan Littlewood's production was the best advertisement for Theatre Workshop that he had yet seen: a model of restraint, integrity, and disciplined naturalism'.

Joan Littlewood had opened the doors of the British theatre to working-class actors. As Harris said, 'There was a tremendous revolution in Britain then. The old establishment, the old upper middle classes, was being kicked aside by people like Finney, O'Toole and myself. John Gielgud said it was frightening. But the great deception was that all we ruffians were also classically trained actors. There was nothing rebellious about our approach.

'The same applies to Clift, Brando and Dean. They were not a new breed of naturalistic actors – they gave highly stylized performances. They painted on their parts with a coat of theatricality that was so special it grabbed us.'

If Behan had stolen the limelight by his colourful behaviour, it was critic Kenneth Tynan who had the final word, '*The Quare Fellow* belongs to theatrical history.'

Harris felt indebted to Joan Littlewood. 'Everything I know and whatever I am supposed to know, I learned from this marvellous lady,' he has said more than once.

The Quare Fellow became a cult play and attracted American and Continental visitors and a host of professional actors and directors, and occasionally Behan himself who turned up at the theatre to ensure that the publicity machine was kept in motion. Once, when he became over-exuberant due to alcohol, the police carried him away protesting. Fleet Street took notice, and the box-office sang a merry song.

Playwright Arthur Miller dropped in to see the play, was impressed by Harris's performance and decided he would be right for the part of the longshoreman in his new play, *A View from the Bridge*. For Harris it was an unexpected break. Social drama appealed to him.

But controversy already surrounded Miller's play and the Lord Chamberlain demanded that one scene, with an emphasis on homosexuality, be cut. Miller objected and it was finally decided to turn the Comedy Theatre into a private members' club for the run of the play. It undermined the Lord Chamberlain's authority – and the censorship law would never again be the same.

With marriage in mind, Harris thought it was time to introduce Elizabeth to his family and friends in Limerick. He was proud of her beauty and, being a showman, he was eager to show her off.

For her part, Elizabeth was anxious to acquaint herself with Richard's Limerick background, the people and streets he so often talked about. And Overdale, the family house, which she felt as though she had known all her life. It was as she expected to find it, large and roomy and situated in a picturesque spot on the Ennis road.

In a leisurely way, he showed her the city's landmarks, the places where he played as a child. All very romantic, she thought, but what else was she to think? He showed her the bedroom where he had been confined during his illness. She noticed that his friends called him 'Dickie' never Richard. Before she left Limerick, she thought, 'Richard has never been allowed into Ireland and Dickie has never left it.'

Stories of his successes in London had by now reached the people of Limerick and they were finally convinced he was an actor, although there was more interest in Elizabeth Rees-Williams than his performance in *The Quare Fellow*. Heads turned in O'Connel Street as he walked arm in arm with her past Crescent College, his old *alma mater*. The *Limerick Leader* published the news of her visit and stories of their intended marriage. No one dared guess who was to be invited to the wedding. The prospect of a London society wedding was rather off-putting to his former pals who wondered if it would be a 'stuffy affair' and not for them.

As always, Harris did not worry about public opinion; as far as he was concerned it would be a family affair. He and Elizabeth had already found a place to live, a small flat in Paddington which would cost them £6 a week.

3 A church wedding

Actor, egotist, raconteur, extrovert, tough guy, potential hellraiser, quintessential Irishman – the description fitted Richard Harris at the beginning of 1957. He was about to cast off the cloak of anonymity for ever, not because he was in the top flight of actors like Olivier, Richardson and Burton, but partly due to his impending marriage to Elizabeth Rees-Williams.

It was a London teeming with actors, Irish included, trying to find a place in the sun. Many would be disappointed. Dubliner Donal Donnelly, a friend of Harris, admitted times were difficult for him as an actor. As he said, 'I managed to live on six pounds a week by working as a waiter or a post-office sorter, but I was unable to act until I found Sunday night work at the Royal Court.'

Unlike Harris, he did not care for London, although he felt it was 'an incredible and fantastic city'. Harris was prepared to settle anywhere as long as he fulfilled his ambition to be a successful actor. In a few years, he had leap-frogged over talented colleagues and by now he was reckoned to have star potential. His individualistic approach, on and off stage, brought him to the notice of directors.

For her part, Elizabeth Rees-Williams, instead of choosing a life of privilege perhaps, had decided to marry the carefree Irishman and continue with her acting. Her decision baffled a few of her best friends. In their eyes, it was a question both of class and nationality. 'Darling, it won't work,' a few of her well-meaning friends cautioned over coffee, as she showed off her engagement ring, which consisted of a large sapphire surrounded by diamonds and fringed by emeralds.

At twenty, she was single-minded and independent. She liked to think she knew what was best for her. The fixed attitudes of others did not unduly worry her. All she knew was that she was passionately in love with Richard, and that was all that mattered to her. Fear of job insecurity or old-fashioned class differences did not make her lose sleep, although she was amused when she reminded others that she came from a family of teetotallers. Harris preferred not to entertain such a sober thought.

It promised to be a stylish and elegant wedding, an event Fleet Street women columnists could scarcely ignore. Having already gained a healthy appetite for publicity, Harris revelled in the popular build-up with its emphasis on glamour and class. The papers were full of what Elizabeth was going to wear. It was in fact a fifty-year-old bridal gown once worn by a great-aunt. Of ivory satin, it was embroidered with fillet and silk lace and silk tassels. The train would be carried by two pages dressed in Irish kilts.

Everyone, including Harris's parents, was pleased that it was going to be a Roman Catholic church wedding. And it was a relief to his friends who feared he might impetuously decide to be married in a London registry office ceremony. In the eyes of his Limerick relatives and friends, some of whom had got invitations to the wedding, the mark of respectability had been ensured by arranging it to be held in a Catholic church. They would settle for nothing less.

As though to put the final imprimatur on the event, *The Times* announced on the morning of Monday, 11 February 1957:

> The marriage took place on Saturday at the Church of Notre Dame de France, Leicester Place, of Mr. Richard Harris, son of Mr. and Mrs. Ivan Harris, of Overdale, Limerick, Eire, and the Hon. Elizabeth Rees-Williams, only daughter of Lord and Lady Ogmore, of 34 Alexandra Court, Queen's Gate, S.W.7, Father Jacquemin officiated and Father Cremin gave an address …

The paper gave further details about the dresses worn by the bridal party, then the report ended with the mundane words, 'A reception was held in the House of Lords.' It seemed an inadequate description, for it was an event in itself. Harris, looking assured and immaculate in a well-fitting dinner jacket, mingled with the three hundred guests as though it were an everyday social occurrence. He joked with earls and politicians, happily introduced his relatives to Elizabeth's aunts, and refused to get ruffled or bored.

Like Laurence Harvey, he loved an audience and here was another unique opportunity for him to perform, even if he must have felt restricted amid the faint air of formality. Nor was the Irish contingent in any way overawed by the sheer grandeur of the House of Lords. Elizabeth would remark later, 'Fortunately, the Irish guests present were not aroused by the Tudor roses that appeared to be carved everywhere; the flavour of the Tudors was strong to my brothers and me. Our parents, so very Welsh, had constantly emphasized our heritage.'

Harris's friends in the business, who tended to envy him his luck, suspected that marriage would not change his personality nor his drinking habits, and wondered if he would be able to provide for his beautiful young bride in the manner expected of him. If confidence counted for anything, then they assumed he probably would in due course. True, he was unpredictable, but he was blessed with a personality and spirit larger than most of his colleagues who were striving for recognition. He was already a name.

That same year Laurence Harvey would marry Margaret Leighton and the publicity surrounding the event almost surpassed that of the Harris wedding; yet while publicity was regarded in the business as sometimes of positive assistance to career advancement the reality was that neither Harvey nor Harris had attained stardom. Harris's bed-sitting-room in Paddington reflected his true status in the business.

The honeymoon was delayed. Harris had to go to the Comedy Theatre to perform in *A View from the Bridge*, and when the play eventually ended its run he was once again faced with the problem of finding work. Money was scarce, though it did help that Elizabeth had joined a repertory company in Blackpool where at weekends she was joined by her husband. It was noticeable that when 'resting' Harris tended to be moody and short-tempered. Donal Donnelly thought, however, that he coped well with the out-of-work periods. 'He was good company,' he recalls, 'and never allowed his spirits to flag. He was an optimist and it paid off.'

Just when it seemed that he would never get work, Joan Littlewood offered him a small part in her modern-dress production of *Macbeth* at Stratford East. All she could afford to pay him for rehearsals was £4 a week.

He wasn't worried. So enthusiastic was he at the offer of playing Shakespeare, that he invited some relatives and friends from Limerick to come to the first night. 'I wanted to show the English how Shakespeare is to be performed ... "Come, come," I said, "everyone come, mother, father, brothers, aunts. The rats from the firm! Be up there in front!" '

The trouble was that he had only about four lines to say and four weeks to rehearse. Came the opening night. Dressed in uniform and sword he had to walk down, utter the four lines, wave his arm, go off stage-right. Suddenly his cue came and he picked up the sword but he couldn't remember a line. 'And I could hear my mother in the front saying "Isn't he marvellous!" '

Miss Littlewood continued though to have faith in his talents. She told him that he was going to star in her next production, *Man, Beast and Virtue* by Pirandello.

'I was petrified,' he says, 'more so because Joan was going to Czechoslovakia to swap places with a man called Franz Yamnick. Yamnick was to direct the Pirandello and I was to read for him the next day. I went home and told Elizabeth that I would never get the part. I am the worst reader in the world. When other players are reading their lines and showing how good they are I am mumbling and not knowing what the hell it is about.'

He was determined not to disappoint the Czech director. There were two parts: a neurotic tutor and a much smaller part, a rough sea captain. He thought that Joan Littlewood had made a mistake about his playing the tutor, so he learned the part of the sea captain. But she hadn't made a mistake; when it came to the reading two of them began to speak the sea captain's part simultaneously.

The reviews of *Man, Beast and Virtue* were generally good. The play was to be transferred to the St Martin's in the West End or the Lyric in Hammersmith; the St Martin's meant waiting for two weeks, but the Lyric meant going in immediately. Business wasn't all that good at the Theatre Workshop, so they opted for the Lyric where the play died a death.

As ever, he was in luck. Director Cliff Owen was preparing a play for television, *The Iron Harp* by Joseph O'Connor, and wanted an Irish actor to play the part of a blind man. Owen had come round by the Lyric on the last night of the Pirandello play and noticed Richard Harris's name on the billboards. He had never heard of the Irish actor so he went inside and caught the last twenty minutes of the performance. Impressed by Harris's appearance on stage, Owen reckoned he might fit the bill. A week later he invited him to read for a part in the television play. Harris is not likely to forget the occasion.

'It was ten minutes to four,' he says, 'and the reading was at four o'clock. We were living in Earl's Court Road at the time, opposite the tube station, but if I was to travel by tube I would not make the appointment. I said to Elizabeth, "Look, I'll have to invest in a taxi fare if I'm not to be late." We broke open the gas meter and I took the money to pay for the taxi. I arrived at the agent's on time and he kept me waiting for over an hour. By then I didn't care if I got the part or not. I could have travelled by tube for sixpence and I had spent ten shillings on a bloody taxi.'

He was furious and turned on the agent. 'I suppose you don't realize what ten shillings means to me,' Harris exploded. 'Ten shillings means four meals for me and my wife and I've spent that money on a taxi to get here.'

The agent was taken aback by the fury of the actor's words and suggested that perhaps he would take the script and read it. A few days later he went back to the agent and got the part. 'I was paid fifty pounds for it,' he says. 'Can you imagine how I felt? I had been earning six pounds a week at the Theatre Workshop.'

He had another stroke of good fortune at this important stage of his career. Bob Lennard showed an interest in him.

A former film and theatre agent, Lennard had influenced the careers of scores of actors, including Richard Todd, Robert Shaw and Laurence Harvey. 'Bob was a man who truly cared for those actors whose careers he was able to influence and assist,' recalled Todd.

He was now casting director for Associated British Pictures, the complex of companies which owned studios at Elstree and the only corporation able to compete with the massive Rank corporation. He had seen Harris's performance in *The Iron Harp* on television and was instantly struck by his screen image.

'He had a presence that suggested star quality,' he said later. 'I could already see him in big screen roles.'

It was Lennard who first discovered Laurence Harvey in Manchester. As he said, 'It was the unusual structure of the young man's face and his enthusiasm on the stage that attracted me.'

Lennard now saw Harris's real future in films. Acting quickly, he arranged a seven-year contract for the actor with Associated British Films which ensured him a salary. Harris said, 'I went to see Lennard with my agent Jimmy Frazer and he agreed to pay me thirty pounds a week for the first year, forty for the second, fifty for the third, and that's how it began.'

For Harris, who had wondered where the next pound was coming from, the regular income was most welcome, particularly with the realization that Elizabeth was expecting their first baby. She had been eager to pursue her acting career, but now decided to postpone it until after the birth. Everything had happened so quickly for them that she did not know what to think.

Harris, who never lacked friends, continued to bring them back home after the pubs had closed. A few of them declined, fearing perhaps that they would not be welcomed at that hour by his wife. Harris was popular among the Irish acting contingent in London and befriended some of them when work was scarce. He had a more extrovert quality than most of his colleagues, could outdrink them, and in the words of Donal Donnelly was 'great company'.

The prospect of film stardom was changing him. With a regular income he was able to spend more nights on the town and his quick temper got him into a few scrapes with the law. Elizabeth saw the change in her husband but seemed unable to stem the tide. He was not a man to listen easily to the advice of others. He could be headstrong and impetuous.

Despite his outgoing ways, he was determined to push ahead with his career in films. Apart from the fact that it paid the best money, he was ambitious enough to want to star in feature films. And he hadn't forgotten Bob Lennard's advice, 'Richard, it's films for you.' Friends worried, though, about the self-destructive forces at work in him and wondered if in time they would destroy the ambitions that promised to make him a star. To them, his capacity for alcohol was sometimes alarming, and his penchant for getting into scrapes ensured his publicity machine would never run down.

However, in more thoughtful moments he was aware that he faced new responsibilities with the forthcoming birth of his first child. But for a man who loved freedom and late nights and conversation, it would take time for the meaning of fatherhood to sink in. He accepted a part in a new film, *Alive and Kicking*, and set out for Scotland, leaving behind a rather anxious Elizabeth.

While Harris was in Oban on film location, Elizabeth stayed with her parents in Kensington. When Fleet Street columnists telephoned her, she could think of little else to say except that she considered the name of Richard's movie a good omen. She hoped he would be back in London before the baby arrived. Lady Ogmore was quoted as saying, 'They do not mind if the baby is a boy or a girl. The baby will be given a Celtic name.'

On Friday, 8 August, *The Times* printed in its Births Column:

Harris – On 2nd Aug. 1958, at Queen Charlotte's Hospital, to Hon. Elizabeth, wife of Richard Harris – a son.

What the paper did not tell readers was the fact that the actor attended the birth and actually fainted at the delivery time.

Curiously the event pinpointed once more the caring and generous side to the actor's character. Intensely proud of being a father, he telephoned his relatives in Limerick as well as his best friends in London. The birth made news in Fleet Street. Harris had become a celebrity while other actors were still struggling for recognition, on and off stage.

Life in his eyes was a celebration and he had no intention of easing up. Colleagues knew he would never be happy until he was a film star in his own right. It was the one thing he had set his mind on, yet he sometimes felt it was a million years off.

Now as he held his baby son Damian in his arms, and smiled into its eyes, he looked no different from any other father. The human side of the actor was apparent to all. No one, however, dared to say that fatherhood would make him more homebound and less gregarious. Before long, his agent was on the line telling him about a film offer that would take him to Dublin.

It was an opportunity that Harris did not care to miss. 'We're going, Elizabeth ... you and me, and the baby.' He said the words with typical enthusiasm, though he knew at that time that Dublin would not exactly be home to him.

4   The Cagney myths

Richard Harris slipped into Dublin unnoticed. To the Irish he was little known as an actor. He was probably best known at that time as the Limerick man who married Lord Ogmore's daughter.

The big fellow wasn't worried. Making headway in his career as a movie actor was far more important to him than anonymity among his own.

Dublin, long recognized as a cinema-going city, was undoubtedly more interested in the arrival from Hollywood of legendary 'bad guy' James Cagney, the star of the new film *Shake Hands with the Devil*, in which Harris had a small part.

Everybody wanted to meet and shake hands with their screen hero. Mindful of the risks to hand and limb, Cagney went into virtual hiding in the plush Shelbourne Hotel. In his own suite he was safely hidden from the gaze of the curious. And the smokescreen that had been laid in his wake was effective but confusing.

When he was confronted one morning by a Sunday-paper columnist, he snapped, 'How did you get in? My publicity man will knock my head off.'

Attired in a plaid dressing-gown, and sporting a small moustache, Cagney reluctantly agreed to talk. 'I play a surgeon in the new picture,' he said in a voice that belied his tough-guy image. 'In a way it is a different part for me. I chose Michael Anderson to direct because I was impressed with his work in *The Dam Busters*. We should finish the shooting in ten weeks.'

United Artists had kept secret the star's whereabouts in the city. An American guest at the Shelbourne said, 'Mr Cagney? Oh, he's in Hollywood!'

At fifty-four, Cagney looked in good shape. For ten years he had been one of Hollywood's biggest money-making stars. With his wife, he now slipped out of the Shelbourne and together they toured the city in a black low-slung Dodge.

Harris, meanwhile, had no need to go into hiding. He rented a small house on the outskirts of the city where Elizabeth and baby Damian settled in quietly. After shooting at Ardmore Studios in Bray, he sometimes entertained friends and colleagues. Never having acted on the stage in Dublin, he was a stranger to most of the Irish he encountered, although some of his Limerick friends dropped in to see him.

Among the cast of *Shake Hands with the Devil* was Cyril Cusack and soon he and Harris had struck up an amiable rapport. 'He became Richard's mentor,' recalled a friend who sometimes saw the actors in deep conversation at the studios.

Cusack had made his debut in the 1940s in Carol Reed's *Odd Man Out* and was a distinguished Abbey Theatre actor. 'In my film parts,' he would say, 'I have concentrated on veracity of characterization. I think my work in films has improved in some ways; it is more solid, less intuitive and perhaps technically better than it used to be.'

Harris was fascinated by Cusack's approach to films, the way he used his voice, which he seldom raised above a certain pitch. They talked about an Irish film industry. Cusack had been quoted as saying:

It worries me that we cannot make our own films. I think this is due to the acceptance of a standard that is wrong for us. I have always believed that it should be possible to produce films in this country economically and artistically and to draw inspiration not from the spectacle films that the Americans produce, but from an original source.

Cusack was impressed by Harris's absorption in films and his unusual determination to be a success. He suggested how he could improve his technique and the best deployment of his voice. For his part, Harris, the younger man by twenty years, respected the other's reputation. 'He was genuinely interested in my career,' he told friends. 'I don't like all actors, but we do get along fine.'

From Hollywood came the young English-born actress Dana Wynter who was under contract to 20th Century-Fox. Tall, slim with limpid brown eyes and classic face, she was cast as the

English woman in the movie. It was the first feature film to be made at Ardmore Studios, and Miss Wynter recalled, 'There was only one sound stage then.'

She was soon struck by the gregarious nature of Harris and considered him 'a character'. It wasn't so funny, though, when they played scenes together.

'Richard came close to putting my eye out,' she says. 'In one scene he had to confront me with a gun and in his over-enthusiasm poked the gun in my eye and nearly knocked it out. Really, I think it was his inexperience as an actor. He was young and film-making was new to him. Of course I forgave him.'

Shake Hands with the Devil was a happy film to make, she said. Everybody was so friendly, and James Cagney was such a generous actor. 'I remember Richard Harris's good humour and boisterous personality. He had a splendid presence on the film set.'

So impressed had Miss Wynter been with the scenic beauty of County Wicklow, that she later returned to make her home there. 'Without making *Shake Hands with the Devil* I don't think I would have discovered Ireland. I saw the potential of film-making at Ardmore Studios. There were young Irish actors like Richard Harris coming along who undoubtedly had star quality and only needed experience.'

Harris was happy to give interviews to the local press and talked openly about his childhood and his hopes of a successful acting career. Photographers snapped Elizabeth and the baby and it could be said she was enjoying her stay in Ireland even if her husband had hardly a spare minute to himself.

He liked working with stars like Cagney and Michael Redgrave, and was prepared to learn. Cagney's professionalism intrigued him – the way he switched himself on when he arrived on the set for the part he was playing. He wasn't surprised, though. The star was reckoned to be very versatile. He seemed capable of playing anything – the tap-dancing vaudeville director or the gang leader, or as he had done, the carefree dentist in the lighthearted *The Strawberry Blonde*.

Harris and the rest of the cast went along to Dublin's biggest theatre, the Theatre Royal for a charity performance in which it was hoped Cagney would perform a famous number from the movie *Yankee Doodle Dandy*. The little man was a sensation, and the 4,000 audience rose to him as he told them stories about his childhood; then he gave a signal to the pit orchestra and instantly they launched into the George M. Cohan song, 'Mary' from *Yankee Doodle Dandy*, the film that had won him an Oscar twenty years before.

It was his last number that provided five minutes of magic, however. He performed the whole of the 'I'm A Yankee Doodle Dandy' song-and-dance routine from the film, complete with intricate taps, pirouettes and high kicks. At the end, the little man waved and smiled at the audience – and was gone.

Harris was learning what was expected of movie stars, wherever they filmed. Presumably they became part of the people, unlike stage actors who tended to be more detached. Screen heroes, he decided, were a different breed. There was an unmistakable aura about them and this was transmitted to their fellow actors. He liked the unique atmosphere surrounding movie-making: the teamwork, the camaraderie, the profession-alism. Although *Shake Hands with the Devil* had been a happy experience, he had no illusions. He had read enough about antagonism on film sets to know what to expect when the time came for him to work with more temperamental stars than James Cagney.

Later, he wasn't worried that *Shake Hands with the Devil*, which was described as 'a fairly preposterous Hollywood version of political events in Ireland', was universally panned by the critics. To Harris, it was his second movie and his performance had received encouraging mention, enough for his agent to comment, 'I think there will be other offers on the way.'

When he packed his bags to leave Dublin he knew that he was still an unknown actor in Irish eyes, but one day he hoped to return a star of either stage or screen. He had no idea when that might possibly happen, nor was he unduly worried.

He was hardly back in London a week when he was offered another picture by director Michael Anderson. It was *The Wreck of the Mary Deare* starring Gary Cooper, to be made in Hollywood.

From childhood, Harris was inclined to see Hollywood through its glittering stars. He read stories about their lives and careers. One summer day in 1949 he was walking down Limerick's

O'Connell Street and as he passed a chemist shop he spied movie star Rita Gam inside. 'I stuck to the ground,' he recalls, 'and must have stared at her for at least five minutes. I waited outside for her to come out and I must admit I was terrified. I had seen her in many movies. I worshipped that woman, I just could not believe it.'

When Miss Gam eventually came out, he walked boldly over to her, put his hand on her shoulder and said, 'Excuse me, aren't you Rita Gam?'

'That's right,' she said surprised. 'Who are you?'

Trying not to tremble, he introduced himself and plucking up courage asked her to join him for a cup of coffee. She explained to him that she was flying to New York and her plane was held up for a couple of hours. He was bowled over by her beauty.

There was one snag – he had no money. He decided to take her to Cruise's Hotel where his brother-in-law Jack Donnelly would provide free coffee. For an hour he chatted to Miss Gam about her career – and Hollywood. Being publicity conscious even then he telephoned the *Limerick Leader* and asked for their show-business columnist Earl Connolly and a photographer to come 'at once to the hotel' for an exclusive.

The following evening the paper ran the story and Harris had acquired, as he said, 'a new name in Limerick'. He reckoned he would be known as the guy who 'laid' Rita Gam. It wasn't quite true but it added to the astonishing number of myths growing up about him. Later, he joked about the experience. 'The reputation was fabulous and all the lads were buying me drinks. I had a completely new image and I was enjoying every minute. The whole of Limerick was talking about my sex frolics with an international movie star.'

The story underlined his deep interest in Hollywood and its movie stars during the forties. It was the glamour that appealed to him, the images presented of the legendary stars, and in some strange way he wanted to be part of the scene. He wasn't sure how it would come about, but already he was drawing a picture in his mind of Beverley Hills and Malibu Beach and the big film studios.

As he prepared to set out that autumn of 1958 for Hollywood, it wasn't quite like that. It was more calculating and he was aware of the work ahead, perhaps the risks involved. Despite his life-long interest in the place, he told himself he really wasn't sure how Hollywood would regard the unknown Richard Harris.

The reality proved painful. Yet it cannot have been altogether unexpected. He was, after all, arriving there an unknown with virtually no friends. Actors from this side of the Atlantic had always found difficulty in settling in a Hollywood where you were either accepted or ignored depending on your status as an actor. Money also mattered, and Harris at that time, despite his busy working schedule, was spending almost more than he was earning. It would have helped enormously though, if he had been able to count among his friends Gregory Peck, Bob Hope, Robert Mitchum and Cary Grant.

Elizabeth summed it up succinctly, 'Richard recognized that Hollywood is entered by many doors and an actor is judged by, and often confined to, his place of entry. It was a baffling, barbed game and we didn't know the rules. And worse than that, there was nobody there to teach us. We didn't even know the right restaurants to get the wrong table in.'

She was correct. They were on the outside looking in, and it wasn't a nice experience. At least the same frustration did not exist in the studios where harmony reigned. Gary Cooper, the star of the movie, was dying of cancer but bravely carried on with his work. He did not shirk the underwater scene which demanded that he be submerged for some considerable time.

The Wreck of the Mary Deare did not exactly get rave notices but it was an important introduction for Harris into a side of Hollywood he was hardly aware existed. He now realized that it wasn't all glamour, that behind the smiles and the limousines there was a detachment that was tangible. 'It was the beginning of Richard's growing up,' says Elizabeth. 'I saw a side of Hollywood that I would never see again.'

The trouble was they had been booked into a motel on the wrong side of town. 'It was weeks before I realized that our glamorous motel wasn't glamorous at all but slightly seedy. Professionally, Richard was up against the wall. His billing on the movie was lowly and his contract protected him barely at all.'

Both were relieved to be sailing for home on the *Queen Elizabeth*. They were able to relax with the company of the passengers and the amenities on board.

Harris was glad to be back in England. He admitted he missed his friends, and, like Elizabeth, baby Damian. It was a vibrant time in the theatre. Brendan Behan was in town for his entertaining new play *The Hostage* at Stratford East and everybody was talking about him and his play. Critic Kenneth Tynan summed up,

> Mr Behan may well fill the place vacated by Sean O'Casey. Perhaps more important, Miss Littlewood's production is a boisterous premonition we all want – a bit of popular drama that does not depend on hit songs, star names, spa sophistication, or the melodramatic aspects of homosexuality.

Harris noted that Joan Littlewood had discovered another important new Irish talent in designer Sean Kenny, whose stage design for *The Hostage* was described by Tynan as 'by far the best in London'.

Harris's egotism grew with his new-found status as an actor. There were ominous signs, sometimes apparent to Elizabeth, that in time it might get out of hand. He treated his friends to drinks and continued to land them back at the house for late-night 'chasers'. His own hangovers were becoming more frequent. Elizabeth said, 'He was determined not to feel trapped in any way.' His outrageous behaviour left her feeling miserable, and there were other times, on her own admission, when it became so overpowering that she felt like giving up.

Suddenly, as though it had never happened, he would be caring and generous, fussing over little Damian. But it was difficult to come to terms with the private and the public Richard Harris; only Elizabeth was aware of all the facets that made up his unusual personality. She was forgiving, though her fiery Welsh temper ensured that he did not get away with everything.

He wanted to get back to the theatre.

5 'Guilty' plea in court

His moving portrayal of the blind man in the TV drama, *The Iron Harp* had prompted one critic to describe him as television's star discovery of 1958. 'Let us see more of Mr Harris,' suggested another critic. It all added up to the fact that Harris was attracting more attention on screen than on stage, and it reinforced Bob Lennard's view that his future lay in screen roles.

But his next appearance would be neither on stage nor screen. He was scheduled to appear in court along with colleagues from Theatre Workshop, Stratford East to answer summonses alleging unlawful presentation of parts of a new play before such parts had been allowed by the Lord Chamberlain.

Surprisingly, one morning paper, the *Daily Express*, commented,

> Every West End star will be watching with keen interest when the case of Richard Harris comes to court. They will be anxious to know how the censorship law, the Theatres Act of 1943, deals with the theatrical facts of life in 1958.

The comment was surprising in view of Harris's standing in the theatre at that time, for he was not a West End star and his reputation fell short of Joan Littlewood's, who was also a defendant in the case. However, it indicated that his name was becoming better known for a variety of reasons, not all of them connected with the theatre.

The case itself was arousing a good deal of public interest and, as ever, Harris revelled in the publicity surrounding this latest *cause célèbre* of the modern theatre. Like the other defendants, including Gerry Raffles, manager of Theatre Workshop, John Bury, theatre licensee, and Henry Chapman, author of the controversial play *You Won't Always Be on Top*, Harris was angry because of the action by the Lord Chamberlain, particularly in view of the fact that on television there was no censorship. For years actors had been asking: why is television free from legislation which binds the theatre?

You Won't Always Be on Top was written by a builder's labourer, and was about the building trade. When the case opened at West Ham Court the public gallery was crowded with actors and actresses from Theatre Workshop Company. The defendants, including Harris, sat silently facing the magistrates.

The court was told that during the performance of the play two officials from the Lord Chamberlain's office had sat in the stalls. The play had three acts and in the second something like 25 or 30 per cent of the matter was in a form never submitted to the Lord Chamberlain. The third was almost completely new – something like 80 or 90 per cent. One of the characters made a speech imitating Sir Winston Churchill and went on to give his version of what Sir Winston would have said if he had been called upon to open a public lavatory.

This caused laughter in the public gallery, but it was noticeable that Harris and the other defendants remained tight-lipped in their seats. Joan Littlewood was the only defence witness called. She told the court:

> The plot was weak, but the thing which won us to it was that for the first time in England I saw written down without taste or discrimination the simple expressions of working men on a building site on a wet Monday morning. And for the first time I heard the speech of the English people put down with such beauty and simplicity as I have never heard before.

Mr Gerald Gardiner, QC, appearing with Mr Harold Lever, MP for the defence said: 'Both Mr Lever and myself appear without fee as admirers of what the company have done for the English theatre.' He said the five defendants pleaded guilty because they knew they had technically broken the law. At this point the QC read a telegram from Alec Guinness which said, 'I am in complete sympathy with your breaking of obsolete censorship law and wish you success.'

There were cheers in court when the defendants were let off with relatively small fines. Harris, and the author of the play, Henry Chapman, were granted conditional discharges on payment of 11s. 6d. costs each. Members of Theatre Workshop and their friends proceeded to make their way to the bar of the Theatre Royal, Angel Lane, where a bowl of daffodils was conspicuous in a corner.

Harris, towering over not a few people in the company, led the way to the bar where he asked for a glass of light ale, a mild drink by his standards. Everyone began to talk about the two men from the Lord Chamberlain's office who had sat in the stalls during the hearing. These were the same two who had taken copious notes at the first night of the play.

Harris had gathered an audience around him. Referring to the men, he said with a shrug, 'It was the underhand way they did it that angers me. The remarks were just asides at the back of the stage. The audience loved it. I think it is just a question of evil in the eye of the beholder.'

He had by now become very much part of the Theatre Workshop scene and his word was respected. He felt he owed a lot to Joan Littlewood who had given him work when it was impossible to open other theatre doors. As a woman of the theatre, she had no equal yet he suspected that in money terms she would never be rich. His philosophy at the time was summed up in his own words, 'I never cared very much about the money I was earning so long as I could eat.'

With film offers coming his way there was now little fear that he would not eat well. When his agent rang him in April 1959 about a movie to be made in Ireland called *A Terrible Beauty* he agreed almost immediately to accept the role of the 'fanatical IRA man'. The cast also impressed him as it included Robert Mitchum, an actor he long admired, Dan O'Herlihy and Cyril Cusack.

To Harris, Ireland meant renewal of friendships, convivial dining out, amusing conversation, jokes, booze and nostalgia. As an actor, he was returning with a growing reputation and not the unknown of *Shake Hands with the Devil*. When he was interviewed by the press, he expressed his admiration for Joan Littlewood.

There was no doubt who was the star of the film. Robert Mitchum's tough-guy image had preceded him across the Atlantic, and in Ireland he was regarded as a Hollywood star. At the same time that Dickie was playing pranks around Limerick in the 1940s, Mitchum's career was taking off and his early career had survived Katherine Hepburn's acerbic remark, 'You know you can't act, and if you hadn't been so good-looking you would never have gotten a picture.'

With his dark-haired good looks, sensuous heavy-lidded eyes and ultra-slow speech, Mitchum stood out from the herd of leading men breaking into movies in the 1940s. His looks and muscular physique had earned him much work in bit parts, and he had appeared in nineteen films in his first year, 1943.

Like Harris, Mitchum was reported to have a short fuse and had learned to take care of himself in a fight. As the cast gathered, a few of them wondered if Harris and Mitchum would be at each other's throats before long. 'At the beginning of the shooting I felt that Mitchum regarded Harris with some suspicion,' recalled Abbey Theatre actor Geoff Golden. 'One or two of his remarks were disparaging, but later on relations improved and they seemed to get on well together.'

Soon after Harris's arrival in Bray, Co. Wicklow he was joined by Elizabeth. 'Richard admired Robert,' she said later. 'He had never met such an open and generous actor before. They got on fine.'

Harris was fascinated by the star's acting style. He would say, 'Don't be taken in by that languorous style of his. He doesn't miss a trick.'

Mitchum quickly established himself as a useful cook. 'He was one of the best in the business,' says Geoff Golden. 'He cooked some splendid meals for us. And he could drink us all under the table.'

After shooting at Ardmore Studios, Harris drank with his pals and the film's crew in the Royal Hotel, Bray. Later, he and Elizabeth and the Mitchums, Robert and his wife Dorothy, would be chauffeur-driven to fashionable eating places in Dublin. Harris, like Mitchum, was a late nighter and could talk into the small hours. Good food appealed to him. Mitchum enjoyed Harris's wild stories, but he gave no indication whether he believed half of them. He became furious, though, when pestered by people for autographs in the dining-room and was known to scribble rude remarks in another star's signature.

Work on the movie continued harmoniously, though producer Raymond Stross was not the most popular individual on the set. Harris, when he found time, chatted with Cyril

Cusack and listened, as he said, 'to the voice of wisdom'. He remained a constant admirer of Cusack, the actor, and counted him his friend.

Dan O'Herlihy had come from Hollywood to play in the movie and saw a change in his native Dublin. 'When you have been out of Ireland for a few years you can romanticize about it; but I have kept coming back and it has stayed in perspective. The wealthy middle-class families of Dublin remind me of the families in San Fernando Valley; the same urges and pushing them to keep up with the Joneses, and they have developed the same tensions.'

Harris did not take such keen notice of Dublin and its citizens. He preferred to retail stories in the pubs; he was restless and was always looking forward to his next project. As Elizabeth said, 'Nothing ever stood still for long with Richard. We could be fighting uncontrollably one hour and the next laughing and loving and full of hope for our future together. I always fell for his charm and his blarney. He could always make me believe that my fears and anxieties were ridiculous and unfounded.'

To his friends, he was great company, generous and witty. Irish actors, who had been slow to accept him when he first arrived to film *Shake Hands with the Devil*, had changed their attitude and felt he 'could have star quality'.

A Terrible Beauty did not set the movie world on fire. Critics found the theme contrived and lacking originality. Harris, however, emerged with favourable personal notices and was satisfied with his own performance.

That August 1959 he was offered the part of O'Keefe in a new play called *The Ginger Man*, adapted for the stage by the author, J.P. Donleavy, from his own novel of the same name. It was due to be presented at the Fortune Theatre, London in September with Jason Robards in the title role.

'That's impossible,' said Harris. 'I should play the Ginger Man. It's me. It's my life.'

He read for the part and got it. Spur Productions even postponed the opening until he had finished *A Terrible Beauty* in Ireland. Harris had read the Donleavy novel and found it raucous, rowdy and very funny. It was based on the rumbustious life of an American named Gainor Crist, who was

attending Trinity College on the GI Bill. Crist was friendly with
Brendan Behan and the poet Patrick Kavanagh and other Dublin
literary characters who lived a bohemian life and were noted
drinkers.

For Harris, the play was important as it afforded him a
starring stage role and kept his name alive in the London
theatre. Bernard Levin found it a rewarding evening, and
commented: 'Richard Harris, as the Ginger Man, Ronald Fraser
as his American fellow-candidate for damnation, Miss Wendy
Craig as his wife, and Miss Isabel Dean as the lodger – each
wears his part as if it were his skin.'

The play was at that time being compared with *Look Back in
Anger*, or, as Levin succinctly put it:

The Ginger Man begins where *Look Back in Anger* left off.
However, Sebastian Dangerfield, the shiftless and dissolute
hero of the Donleavy work, makes Jimmy Porter look like a
Stakhanovite. Like Jimmy, Dangerfield is eternally seeking,
and knows he will never find. Drowned in debt and dirt and
drink, he can yet pop his head out to jeer at fate and spit in
salvation's eye.

'We got seventeen curtains on the opening night and received
incredible notices,' recalls Harris, 'and the theatre was full
despite a General Election and a heatwave.'

The *Sunday Express* critic, though, found the play 'a
depressing evening in the theatre' and described its hero as 'an
idle, drunken, dreaming, raucous and bawdy Dublin student.
As played by Richard Harris the Ginger Man is a fraudulently
just-sympathetic character: a hulking baby unable to come to
terms with his own intelligence'.

Harris was finding the play an exhilarating experience. And
he had the last lines to say each night:

God's mercy
On the Wild
Ginger Man

The lines were appropriate during the run of the play, for at
night he 'lived it up' and there were times when his friends
believed he was determined to be the Ginger Man, on and off

the stage. The hellraiser in him was beginning to cut loose, yet every evening he arrived in his dressing-room at the Fortune Theatre sober and terribly anxious to improve on his previous performances. Acting to him was a serious business, and he was still fired by ambition; life continued to be a wild celebration. The only question that worried his friends was whether he could control the self-destructive forces threatening to engulf him.

Elizabeth Harris, who was trying to hold together a shaky marriage, was only too aware of his wild behaviour. 'Had Richard left his performance on stage after the final curtain, all would have been well. Unfortunately, somewhat obsessed by Stanislavsky and all the talk of the Actors' Studio in New York at that time, he continued to live the grotesque Dangerfield off stage. With the characters he liked playing, he assimilated them into his own life for the duration of the play or film.'

6   *Shock for the Ginger Man*

Harris opened his dressing-room door to Godfrey Quigley, actor/manager of Dublin's Globe Company, and both men warmly shook hands. Quigley complimented him on that night's performance and told the actor it was the first time he had seen him on stage.

'Would you do *The Ginger Man* in Dublin?' he asked Harris.

'I'd love to, Godfrey.'

Quigley, a big, friendly theatre man, was impressed by the depth and vigour of Donleavy's writing, and the well-drawn characterization. He was also influenced by the fact that he knew Gainor Crist, the *real* Ginger Man, and drank with him.

The London run was coming to an end. Before he left the dressing-room Quigley said, 'I'll play O'Keefe in the Dublin production, Dickie.'

He preferred to call him Dickie rather than the slightly formal Richard. Harris did not mind. When Quigley returned to Dublin he went to see Louis Elliman, the owner of the Gaiety Theatre, and a member of one of the best-known Jewish families in the city.

'How about us doing *The Ginger Man* here, Louis?' he asked.

Elliman drew on his cigar and said, 'Do you think it's worth doing, Godfrey?'

'I do. It has a lot going for it in Dublin. And the London notices were good, you know.'

The play would be presented at the Gaiety Theatre by Spur Productions Ltd., in association with the Globe Company. Quigley admitted that the Globe had less than a thousand pounds in the bank but he was not worried about the risk factor as he believed *The Ginger Man* would pack for the three-week run.

Except for the Harris role of the Ginger Man, the play was

Outside the church of Notre Dame de France, Leicester Square, in February 1957: Richard Harris leaves his first wedding ceremony with the twenty-year-old actress daughter of Lord and Lady Ogmore, Elizabeth Rees-Williams.

Richard and Elizabeth Harris arrive at the Odeon cinema, Leicester Square, in February 1963 for the première of *This Sporting Life*.

The Harrises at play with their three small sons, Damian, Jared and Jamie, in their London home.

On location in Mexico for *Major Dundee* (1965) – with producer Jerry Bressler.

Two screen tough guys (Harris with Kirk Douglas) plough through the snows of Norway while on location for the £2 million war film *The Heroes of Telemark*.

A brush with the law: Harris arrives at Bow Street Court after an incident the previous evening.

At Hollywood in 1958 for the making of *The Wreck of the Mary Deare* with Gary Cooper.

Heathrow airport, 1970:
Harris setting a new trend for
men's fashion – the
sheepskin maxi coat!

Harris arrives with a friend at
the Royal European charity
première of *Camelot* at the
Warner, Leicester Square, in
November 1967.

Rachel Roberts co-starred in
Harris's first major movie,
This Sporting Life (1963).

Harris directed and starred in *Bloomfield*
(1970), the story of a footballer on the
decline.

A *tour de force* – as the eponymous hero of
Cromwell (1970).

With Romy
Schneider in
Bloomfield.

Kirk Douglas and Richard Harris have always proved a volatile combination!

Vanessa Redgrave, Harris's co-star in the big-budget Hollywood musical version of *Camelot*.

recast. Quigley would play O'Keefe; Genevieve Lyons the role of Marion Dangerfield, his wife; and Rosalie Westwater would portray Miss Frost. Harris was aware that Dublin theatre had a history of controversy and he could recall the sordid case of *The Rose Tattoo*, which ended in a court hearing, and O'Casey's *The Drums of Father Ned*, a year later in 1958, when the Catholic Archbishop of Dublin, as well as O'Casey, the Globe Company and the Dublin Theatre Festival, got locked together in a messy little dispute.

Somewhere in the back of his mind he had a funny feeling about *The Ginger Man*. As he said, 'From what I had heard about the Dublin theatre I suppose I thought there might be fun.'

The first night was fixed for Monday, 26 October 1959. On Sunday morning J.P. Donleavy flew into Dublin on the same plane as Harris and the play's director, Philip Wiseman. The playwright had attended the closing night at the Fortune Theatre and backstage, after the final curtain, said goodbye to the players, later retiring to a nearby pub where the bar was awash. Next morning, on his own admission, he was not in a fit condition to take the plane to Dublin, but he had no other option.

That Sunday night, Harris joined the rest of the cast for a rehearsal in a small hotel reception room. At 10 p.m. Donleavy dropped in.

'I pushed open the doors,' he recalled. 'I saw tired people going through movements and lines over and over again. In the room there were two chairs and a carpet. The floor trembled as Richard Harris struck his forehead with the palm of his hand when a line slipped his mind. Philip Wiseman squatted, seated on his heel as Harris said, "Don't tell me, don't tell me, whatever you do." Then the line would come and relief to the watching faces. Afterwards, all of us adjourned for refreshments, a pot of thick rust-coloured tea.'

On Monday morning the papers carried an announcement of the opening that evening of *The Ginger Man*. In one hotel a red and white placard hung by the reception desk saying, 'Nightly at eight p.m., The Dublin play that startled London. Richard Harris, in *The Ginger Man*'.

It was barely five years since he had left Limerick; now he was back in Dublin topping the bill. Relatives and friends in Limerick were planning to be at the first night. In the lobby of Jury's

Hotel, J.P. Donleavy wrote notes of good wishes to Harris and the cast.

By the time the curtain rose at eight o'clock, the theatre was full, and Act I proceeded without any hint of protest from the audience. The setting for Act II was the sitting-room of a suburban house. Marion Dangerfield is arranging flowers. The front doorbell rings. Marion opening the door, looks and slams it shut. The voice of Dangerfield from outside.

DANGERFIELD: Please let me in for God's sake, Marion. I say, Marion, are you alone? Really, this is ridiculous behaviour. You can't do this.
The window opens. Dangerfield wearing a bowler hat, scrabbling in
MARION: Why don't you leave me alone? You desperate bastard.

Harris, as Dangerfield, was on stage for most, if not all of the play. A marathon role by any standard. Donleavy's lines drew laughter from the audience and the response, as a whole, was warm. It was rumoured at the interval that plain-clothes police were taking notes of some of the lines. To Donleavy, it appeared an ominous sign. Was there trouble in store?

Shortly after the curtain rose on Act II, a voice was heard to shout from the parterre, 'This has gone far enough.' This was followed by some boos and jeers. But the remark was not taken up and the play proceeded as before with sporadic applause from the audience. At the final curtain there was prolonged and enthusiastic applause. The plain-clothes police officers put their notebooks away and vanished into the night.

Harris went back to his dressing-room which was shortly to fill up with relatives and friends from Limerick. Donleavy and Philip Wiseman sauntered into the Gaiety bar for drinks. It was full, with first-nighters discussing the play. 'Where's the Ginger Man?' asked one raised voice, meaning Gainor Crist, the Dangerfield in the play.

Godfrey Quigley, who was about to hurry to his dressing-room, was suddenly approached at the side of the stage by Louis Elliman, who was accompanied by a Franciscan priest.

'What a great show we had tonight, Godfrey,' said Elliman, lighting up a cigar.

'I'm glad you thought so, Louis.'

After a slight pause, Elliman said, 'Well, there are a couple of things we've got to cut for the rest of the run, Godfrey.'

Quigley looked surprised.

'Oh! ... is there? ... What are they, Louis?'

'You'll have to cut out that reference to the church on the Quays, and the lines about Dingle.'

Quigley told him that he considered it a very serious development, and added, 'I better call our director Philip Wiseman.' He called over to (the Jewish) Wiseman and asked Elliman to repeat what he had already said about the cuts.

'I'm cutting nothing,' snapped Wiseman. 'The play remains as it is.'

Quigley knew there was already talk of taking the play to Broadway. Before he departed the stage, Elliman turned to Wiseman. 'You are going to cut that or I'm going to close the show. What's more, I'll see you never work in America.'

Quigley found it amusing that the two Jewish gentlemen were at each other's throats. The whole thing was ludicrous, particularly the cuts Elliman was demanding. How could he see harm in the reference to Dingle:

Down in Dingle
Where the men are single
Pigwidgeon in the closet
Banshee in the bed
An antichrist is suffering
While the Gombeen man's dead
Down in Dingle.

The demand for cuts in Act II, Scene ii arose out of a seduction scene between Dangerfield and the lodger Miss Frost, who complains bitterly, 'It's a mortal sin. And you made me, Mr. Dangerfield. Oh God, I shouldn't have let you put your mattress next to mine.'

DANGERFIELD: Miss Frost, God is merciful.

MISS FROST: But it's a mortal sin which I have to confess to the priest, and it's adultery.

DANGERFIELD: Fear not. There's a special church on the
     Quays where you confess these things. I'll find out for you.

At that time there was a well-known Franciscan church on the
Quays where men and women went to get absolution for their
mortal sins. Quigley felt that Elliman, being a Jew, was trying to
avoid any clash with the Catholic Church, particularly the
Franciscans. He felt it was absurd on Elliman's part to read so
much into the scene.

Later, when Donleavy was interviewed about the cuts
demanded, he pointed out that Dangerfield never mentioned a
church on City Quay but referred to the church on the Quays.

Harris meanwhile was busy shaking hands with his folk from
Limerick. 'So you've all come,' he said happily. He did not
overhear Wiseman say to Donleavy, 'They want us to cut the
show.'

The playwright looked at Wiseman incredulously. 'Whoops!'
he exclaimed.

Wiseman said, 'I told Mr Elliman there were to be no cuts in
this show. That we have a contract with the author to this effect.'

The play got mixed reviews next morning. The *Irish Times* critic
thought that the production and acting took much of the credit.

Richard Harris, in the central part is brilliant. It's a part which
     demands extraordinary physical and emotional reserves ...
     While Donleavy's novel brought down the wrath of the
     French Government on its publishers, last night's stage
     presentation brought only a few shouts from the audience.

The *Irish Press* critic commented, '*The Ginger Man* is slightly
lunatic, more than slightly brilliant and considerably distaste-
ful.' However, he found the second act seduction scene 'the
most offensive ever performed on a Dublin stage'. Richard
Harris's performance was magnificent, at times, he added, but
very often his antics were boring and exaggerated.

To everyone's surprise there was no review in Ireland's
biggest-selling daily, the *Irish Independent*. The cast, including
Harris, had that Tuesday morning assembled in the Green
Room of the Gaiety, where each was reading a newspaper
review of the play.

'Well, what's going to happen?' Harris asked. 'Are we going on, or aren't we? Whatever you do, I'll play it. I'll go on a soapbox on O'Connell Bridge, if necessary. Just let me know when there's a decision.'

Philip Wiseman announced there was no change in his decision not to cut the play. Later, Godfrey Quigley came into the room with the *Evening Herald*. It was a damning review. 'The pace of the play is murderously like a film in slow motion,' it said. 'Richard Harris acts authoritatively in the title role.'

The *Evening Mail* described the play as 'most tasteless, trivial and empty' and the critic was uncomplimentary about Harris's performance.

Harris formed the impression that Donleavy would be willing to cut the play for the sake of keeping it on, but he himself did not see why cuts should be made when they had not been given an official reason by any particular body. 'We learned from Louis Elliman that he had been asked to make the cuts,' he recalled. 'We knew that a Father McMahon, who was secretary to the Catholic Archbishop of Dublin, had been in Elliman's office and backstage, so we assumed that the approach had come from him. If I remember rightly they wanted to cut the references to Confession, and maybe my attitude to crucifixion at the end of the first act was on their list.'

Harris wanted to defy them. 'I had received messages, unofficially and indirectly, that as a Catholic I should not appear in plays of this nature. I telephoned Father McMahon and asked him why he thought the play was anti-Catholic and why I should not appear in it. I asked him to tell me specifically what was wrong with the play and what references were offensive to the Catholic Church. He answered "Go and speak with your spiritual advisor," and hung up.'

With eight minutes to go to curtain-up on Tuesday night, Louis Elliman was addressing a delegation in his dressing-room that included Philip Wiseman. Elliman said, 'There are people out there tonight, waiting to get into this theatre, I don't care. I'll turn them away if I must; these are reasonable cuts you are being asked to make. If I saw this play in London, I would never have agreed to put it on in this city.'

After a pause, he asked, 'Gentlemen, are you going to make these cuts?'

There was no reply. Suddenly the manager in evening dress was at the door. He peeked his head in at one minute to eight. 'Raise the curtain, the show goes on,' declared Elliman.

The *Irish Independent* sent along its representative 'D R', who next morning reported,

> The current production in the Gaiety of *The Ginger Man* is one of the most nauseating plays ever to appear on a Dublin stage and it is a matter of some concern that its presentation should ever have been considered. It is an insult to religion and an outrage to normal feelings of decency ...

Harris looked in vain for his own name and that of the cast in the review. Donleavy, who had got a copy of the newspaper late on the previous night, hurried to Jury's Hotel and straight to bed. 'There was a sense of something, a black wire cage being wound around me,' he recalled. 'And I lay myself down to sleep a little fitful in this unhappy land.'

Philip Wiseman wrote to the editor of the *Irish Independent* and complained that its critic's review of *The Ginger Man* was 'a deliberate attempt to incite a breach of the peace'.

Godfrey Quigley noticed that Harris was enjoying the controversy. 'Dickie was hungry for publicity,' he remembers, 'and regaled the world's pressmen with stories in the Baily bar. He loved holding court in that way and people listened to him. I admired his energy, for I was already feeling the strain of the whole business.'

That Wednesday, Harris dropped into Jury's Hotel and shared a drink and sandwiches with Donleavy. He reminded the playwright of previous theatrical controversies in Dublin. It didn't matter that the actor exaggerated the stories of 'damage' to theatres and 'burnings and beatings'. Harris was restless and puzzled by the attitude to *The Ginger Man* and the wonder then was that he had the stamina left to play at all at night in the Gaiety Theatre.

That night there was, in Quigley's view, an eerie feeling about the theatre. 'We were told by the management that tonight is the last performance of *The Ginger Man*. After that, the theatre will close.'

Harris and the rest of the cast knew it was the last night. The audience, as before, was enthusiastic and Quigley had no doubt that if allowed to run the play would make money for the Globe.

'I wasn't angry when it finished,' said Harris. 'In fact, I was sorry when it came off because I was enjoying it.'

The play would have been retained if Philip Wiseman had agreed to make cuts. As it was, *The Ginger Man* made theatrical history in Dublin, being the first play to be stopped.

One newspaper headline summed up the controversy: 'THE GINGER MAN OFF AFTER THREE NIGHTS'.

Harris confided in Donleavy, 'This play has ruined my life and health, wrecked my marriage and nearly killed me. But I think it's a classic.'

The actor was near exhaustion and his stormy marriage was at crisis point. But he was able to join the 'mourners' in the Baily bar, where Brendan Behan was holding court. 'This is a sad day for this country,' said the playwright. 'My uncle wrote the National Anthem and he might just as well have written "We Ain't Got No Bananas".'

Patrick Kavanagh raised his voice above the din to remark, 'The city's alive. Breathing. Donleavy's taken over, where Yeats and the rest failed. The city lives again.'

Harris decided to send a message to the Archbishop's secretary. It read, 'Your Grace, I have been invited to play the part of the Ginger Man in New York. Will you advise me spiritually whether I should go ...?' Within an hour the messenger returned to the Baily with a reply for Harris, saying, 'Dear Mr. Harris, his Grace has asked me to tell you to seek advice from your spiritual confessor ...'

The actor roared with laughter and both Behan and Kavanagh joined in. Donleavy dropped in to say goodbye to the folks there. In the car to the airport Harris slept while Wiseman was 'too polite to ask for a reduction in speed'.

In Limerick *The Ginger Man* episode had caused the Harris family some embarrassment. Ivan Harris, the actor's father, felt ashamed of the publicity surrounding the play and the involvement of the Catholic Church.

The *Limerick Leader* decided to ignore it. When one of the paper's young reporters asked if he should telephone Richard Harris and get a story for the paper, he was told by the chief reporter, 'Please don't bother. We don't want anything about *that* scandalous play.'

The veteran editor, Con Cregan, was not greatly surprised by Richard Harris's involvement in the production. He still regarded the actor as 'eccentric' and he admitted he did not understand 'the poor fellow'.

Nonetheless, the Limerick contingent who did attend the play at the Gaiety Theatre regarded it as fun but by no means a great play. They were more interested in meeting the *new* Dickie Harris, film and stage actor. To them he hadn't changed. He was as generous as ever and retailed as usual a few amusing stories about growing up in Limerick.

They refused to condemn him.

For Godfrey Quigley, the closure of the play was a traumatic experience. His company, the Globe, stood to lose £8,000, but he was able to meet his commitments to London's Spur Productions Ltd, and Louis Elliman did not hold the Globe to its contract. 'I probably lost in all about £800 but the Globe could not afford that much.'

To Quigley, the ball was bouncing for Richard Harris and the young Limerick actor loved the excitement and controversy the play generated in Dublin. Although he considered him a convincing Ginger Man, he felt that Harris lacked that 'dangerous quality' needed for the stage character.

'I thought that the image he presented of the man was not nasty or tough enough. I knew Gainor Crist well and drank with him and he was an abrasive individual. Donleavy's stage version was a romantic conception. I could appreciate why Dickie Harris wanted to play him. He identified with him.'

7 'My wife has left me'

The role of the Ginger Man had come between Harris and his wife Elizabeth.

Elizabeth had gone back with little Damian to her parents and threatened divorce proceedings against her husband. The red-haired actor was too exhausted to cope with the latest marital crisis in his life. 'I have to go into a home,' he announced wearily. 'My doctor says that unless I take a rest he will take no responsibility for my health.'

He admitted that *The Ginger Man* had broken his marriage. 'My wife has left me. She complains that I've been living the part of the Ginger Man. I have to rid my system of the Ginger Man.'

For two weeks he rested in a Cornish nursing home and afterwards returned to London looking refreshed. Colour had come back to his cheeks and his eyes were alert again. He had desperately tried to put the Ginger Man from his mind.

By now Elizabeth and Damian had moved into a flat in Allen House, off Kensington High Street, but during the separation Harris stayed in a bachelor flat. He cut a lonely figure. The position was made worse by news from Limerick that his mother was dying of cancer. They had always been close and she forgave him when others didn't. 'She invariably saw the good side of her son,' a friend in Limerick recalled, 'and although she rebuked him when he was troublesome she utterly believed in him. Dickie's success later gave her a great deal of happiness.'

Harris travelled immediately to Limerick; Elizabeth followed shortly afterwards, and the inevitable reconciliation took place. Once more she saw the gentle side to the man; those caring characteristics that made a mockery out of his outrageous behaviour. He was unrecognizable as the Richard Harris capable of throwing a chair in rage across a sitting-room, or lashing his wife with his tongue, or making little of her parents. The paradox was that he could be an entirely different individual when it suited him. Elizabeth never ceased to be baffled by the mystery.

'Dickie was very broken up over his mother's illness,' recalls Tom Stack, a former Crescent College colleague, who met him on the train to Limerick. 'I used to visit the Harris house and I knew how much he loved his mother.'

Harris joined his brothers in her room as she lay dying. It was a moving spectacle as he held her hand and whispered to her. For days he hardly slept a wink. When she died, he was crestfallen, a man in a dream.

To Elizabeth, it was a touching experience. She saw the big man grieve silently. Later she would say, 'Richard loved his mother deeply. It was a remarkable relationship and I didn't begin to understand it until it had ended.'

Despite his success in the business, he was still fond of playing pranks. 'He never lost his love of mischief-making,' remembers a Limerick friend who occasionally stayed with him in Allen House. 'He was alive and funny. Once he walked into a posh lady hairdressers in Kensington High Street and put a handkerchief over his face and announced it was a hold-up. The women stared at him in alarm. He then picked up a lovely black ebony bust of a woman on a stand and ran into the street with it. The hairdressers were at the door shouting after him, but of course he returned the bust a few minutes later. On other occasions, he'd kick barrels in the street late at night, or remove statues, but he always returned them. It was Dickie's way of letting off steam.'

To others who knew him well, it was also his way of stirring the placid social waters, or even perhaps taking a kick at the establishment. Drunk or sober, he liked to play pranks. He was prepared at a moment's notice, provided someone sponsored him, to climb the tallest mountain in Britain. Or participate in a competition for the best pint drinkers. In his eyes it was fun, nothing else. He still continued to be generous to out-of-work Irish actors in London, but Fleet Street columnists sometimes found him madly unpredictable.

On one occasion, he gave a Sunday paper columnist a lengthy

interview on tape, retailing some of his most colourful stories, but next day asked the journalist to 'scrub it'. In that way he made enemies among the media but it didn't worry him.

Harris was also inclined to stage-manage his own interviews. He became a master of leading interviewers through a merry dance of dazzling tales and anecdotes which, though entertaining, rarely revealed more than peripheral truths about the man. He was fond of saying that 'truth can be dull'.

It was noticeable that despite his pranks, drinking and waywardness, his ambition as an actor was as strong as ever, and his approach was certainly more professional. Film offers continued to come his way. He joined the cast at Elstree for work on *The Long and the Short and the Tall*. Apart from Richard Todd and Richard Harris, there was Laurence Harvey, whose performance as Joe Lampton in *Room at the Top* had made him a star.

With its powerful realism and engaging insights into sex and class, the theme appealed to Harris. Class was a tangible commodity in Britain and he was aware that it was present in his own marriage to Elizabeth. Years later, he stated, 'The British consider the Irish as working-class whatever we do or whatever status or part of society we come from. We're all peasants to them. They stamped me as that. I wasn't going to argue. If they want to think that, let them think it.'

He was aware, nonetheless, that class, however it was defined, was no barrier to the advancement in his own career. At that time he was grouped alongside Finney and O'Toole as people who came from 'basic working-class families'. The success of *Room at the Top* was based on the breaking down of class and wealthy social structures and Harris admitted that Harvey had carried off the role of Joe Lampton extremely well.

The rugged Harris lacked Harvey's sophistication and urbanity, yet the two men hit it off splendidly at Elstree, ate and drank together, and shared, it seemed, the same dislike for the aloof Richard Todd. 'He's not one of us, Richard,' Harvey would remark as Todd stayed on his own. Harris emerged from the movie with honour and impressed Carl Foreman enough to land a part in *The Guns of Navarone*.

It was a small role for him but the money was good and he was joining established stars Gregory Peck, David Niven, Anthony Quayle and Anthony Quinn. A proud actor, Harris, while he respected veteran stars, was never one to be overwhelmed by reputations. He hated pretension, bigheadedness and bullshit. He learned that *Navarone* had been in preparation for a year and the interior shooting would be at Shepperton Studios and on location on the island of Rhodes.

A week before work began, there was a hitch. Director Alexander Mackendrick was fired and was shortly afterwards replaced by J. Lee Thompson. Playing the mountain-climber, Peck was to emerge as the film's leader, partly as a result of the plot and partly because he was that much bigger a star than any of the others.

Based on a commando assault on a Greek island in wartime 1943, Peck was to remark, 'None of us took it over-seriously and everyone got on well together.'

It was true to a point, because Anthony Quinn was not always easy to get on with. '*Navarone* was a very long film and we were a very mixed bunch of people,' agreed Anthony Quayle. While Harris enjoyed working with Peck and Quinn, he still yearned for a big, starring role that would provide him with the same scope as Harvey enjoyed in *Room at the Top*. He would continue to feel frustrated until the offer arrived on his table.

Meanwhile, he was pleased to be part of the *Navarone* success. What made the film compulsive viewing in the cinema was the macho image presented of the commandos and the tension created in the assault on the German units. As Gregory Peck explained, 'There were 550 chances for them to kill us before we even set foot on the island, but we had to do it with total conviction, even though we were aware that it was flirting with parody.'

The movie cost an unprecedented six million dollars to make, but took just over twice that in the first year of its American release. Critics claimed that it started a vogue for all-star international action-adventure pictures which was to last for at least two decades.

On his return to London, Harris was offered the role of a mutineer by MGM in a remake of the epic *Mutiny on the Bounty*. The film starred Trevor Howard – and Marlon Brando, the actor he had once liked to mimic in scenes from *On the Waterfront*.

8   *Mutineer on the Bounty*

You know, *Mutiny on the Bounty* almost made me a drunk and a tramp. It was disgusting. But I survived. I survived and made myself a promise. I promised myself that however poor I got I would never again do anything I didn't really believe in.

He was already proving a 'quotable' source for columnists, but after only six movies it seemed too early to make promises. Harris's detractors claimed that his words were partly prompted by his personality clash with Marlon Brando and also because he turned out to be a poor sailor – he got seasick aboard the rocking *Bounty*. At the time, it seemed over-reaction on his part, curious coming from an actor who did exceptionally well in what was really a major supporting role and should arguably have been considered for an Academy Award as Best Supporting Actor.

He was now being described as tough, dedicated, and nonconformist in dress and behaviour. It was his first meeting with Brando and he was wary of him, but not overawed by his reputation. Looking back, Harris says, 'I caused problems on only one movie in my life. During *Mutiny on the Bounty* I stood up to Marlon Brando at a time when a whole industry cowed and crumbled before him. I called him a gross, misconceived, bloody animal. That was a legendary row and it's lived with me ever since. But even John Huston, when asked what it was like working with Harris said, "The next time I read he's caused problems on a film I'll be forced to believe it's because the director or producer hasn't done his homework." '

News was emanating at that time from Tahiti, where *Mutiny on the Bounty* was being shot on location, of growing tension and clashes among the stars. When Noel Purcell, the tall, white-bearded veteran Irish actor flew into Dublin from Tahiti, he was instantly quizzed by reporters. 'Sure Harris and Howard are mad with Brando,' he said, 'but at the end of the day they'll make up and turn in a damn good movie.' Purcell, a survivor of a dozen sea movies, added 'Take it from me folks, Dickie Harris is going to be a star after this.'

It was no secret that MGM were paying him the biggest fee he had got up to then for a movie, and he was guaranteed equal billing with Trevor Howard, which in itself seemed a somewhat presumptuous request on Harris's part. To the actor, this was his golden opportunity. His motto was, *if they want me that bad, let them pay for me.*

Filming was set to begin on 15 October 1961. Sir Carol Reed, whose career badly needed a boost, was asked to direct. He accepted but insisted that Trevor Howard play the vicious Captain Bligh, leaving Brando to portray Fletcher Christian. By now 7,000 islanders had been recruited to appear in the film. Harris, who had travelled to Tahiti alone, was accommodated in a small hut and when the torrential rains came and stopped shooting, the conditions were pretty miserable.

Soon disappointment about the script arose and shooting was again held up. There was also a problem with the light since it was changeable, and a sequence that began at sea would have to be cancelled because of an instant downpour. The *Bounty* itself, which had been built in Nova Scotia for $750,000, was becoming dangerously top-heavy with cameras, cables and crew, and she 'rocked around like a cork on the waves'.

In the evenings, Harris, Howard and some of the crew members drank in the island taverns. Others found the beautiful local girls irresistible. Assistant director Reggie Callow remarked, 'You could meet one of these girls at Papeete's Grand Hotel, and half an hour later you were home in bed with her. Some of the girls even moved in with crew members and actors; a man could be taking a shower and suddenly see a young beautiful girl standing naked in the bathroom doorway, announcing that she was the maid.'

There was by now increased talk of a clash between Carol Reed and producer Aaron Rosenberg. As the director continued to demand changes in the script in line with his own conception of the movie, the producer lost patience and fired him, to the consternation of Harris, Howard and Hugh Griffiths. It was said that Brando regretted seeing him go. He was replaced by Lewis Milestone who, years before, had directed *All Quiet on the Western Front*.

Frustrated because there was no satisfactory ending to the script, Brando took solace in the company of a lovely young girl named Tarita who was cast, ironically, as his girlfriend in the story. They soon became off-screen lovers.

The star tended to keep aloof from the other actors and the crew noticed that he was not friendly with Harris; the feeling seemed mutual. Trevor Howard was becoming more miserable every day and once while out drinking with Harris and Griffiths 'disappeared', but a few hours later was spotted by a local police wagon and returned to base.

To Milestone, the movie was turning into a nightmare. 'I knew we were going to have a stormy passage right away,' he reflected later. 'I like to get on with things, but Brando likes to discuss every scene, every line for hours. I felt enough time had been wasted, but time didn't seem to mean anything to Brando. He argued about every scene. When eventually the arguments were over, I'd be told Brando was ready for the cameras. It was a terrible way to make a picture.'

Harris now felt that a clash with Brando was inevitable. It came, appropriately enough, in a fight scene. Brando had to hit him and bowl him into a camp fire. He said his lines and then tapped Harris lightly on the side of the face, but the actor stayed firmly on his feet. He then told the astonished director, Lewis Milestone, that he would fall down when Marlon Brando hit him hard enough to make it look realistic.

Brando then repeated his feather blow. Impulsively, Harris stepped forward and planted a kiss on the star's cheek. Milestone went pale, expecting Brando to erupt. But he remained strangely calm, his blows becoming no heavier. As though to mock him, Harris whispered, 'Shall we dance?'

Brando became enraged, but he still refused to increase the force of his punches. Milestone threw up his hands in horror and called it a day.

For hours afterwards, the episode was the chief topic among the crew. Harris joined Howard for a drink and advised him 'not to be walked on' by Brando. Up to then Howard had shown unusual patience in face of provocation.

The next morning the scene was again more like something aboard the HMS *Pinafore* than HMS *Bounty*. Milestone seemed utterly incapable of directing Brando to do it his way. In disgust, Harris shrugged his shoulders and walked off, but not before he had used a few colourful frothy words to his co-star.

The film shut down for five days of agitated argument. Two reasons meanwhile were put forward for Brando's reluctance to play the scene the Harris way. 'For some reason, Marlon couldn't bring himself to do this,' argued one American observer. 'Perhaps he was afraid that in view of his feelings for Harris, he might cause him real injury. Instead he just barely tapped him.'

Harris's theory was that the scene was repugnant to Brando because it made him look a heavy. Trevor Howard was not greatly surprised by Harris's show of temperament; he had expected some trouble when he signed to do the movie. He had been warned that Brando always tried to run every film he'd been in and would probably try to do the same in *Mutiny*. With the unexpected departure of Carol Reed, he feared the worst.

The first scene between Howard and Brando gave a true indication of what was to come. It was Howard's scene, with five pages of dialogue for him and a few words for Brando. Every time he hit his lines, Brando fluffed. They went on for eight takes. Then, when Brando felt that the other might be off-key he threw his line back. It was regarded as 'a dirty trick' in the actor's manual and Brando had performed it. The crew couldn't believe that Howard wouldn't 'do a Harris' and put Brando in his place. It might have saved the actor many hours of inner torment and bitter frustration.

Elizabeth Harris was pregnant when she arrived in Tahiti with her son Damian. Richard, she found, was thrilled with the news that their second child was due. They took a house on the island with a picturesque view and soon were entertaining actors and crew on the set.

She had already read stories about tension and arguments and wondered how true they were. She soon became aware of what was wrong. As she said, 'All was not well on the picture. There were so many people blaming people.'

Since Brando's name figured in most of the 'battle reports' from Tahiti, she had looked forward to meeting the star. She found he was a man who never gave a clue to what he was really thinking. There was a sense of isolation about him nearly all the time. He carried a book most of the time which suddenly engrossed him whenever he wished to avoid conversation. He and Richard, she noted, never seemed to relax together. 'Richard kept his distance,' she recalled. 'Still, he admired Marlon as an actor.'

Elizabeth's arrival had helped to make life on Tahiti more tolerable for Harris. Something else also greatly helped. He was approached from London with an offer to star in a new movie called *This Sporting Life*. They sent him David Storey's novel and he liked it immensely.

As he said, 'I was in a state of absolute desperation at the time, what with Brando's behaviour and the film dragging on interminably I didn't know where to turn. Suddenly, I get this novel and I'm a new man. I found a tremendous affinity with it but the first script was terrible. I didn't even answer that letter.'

The director of the film, Lindsay Anderson telephoned to say he was arriving in Tahiti to work with him on the script. Anderson, who had not known Harris, felt he was the actor for the leading part. 'For three weeks we worked night and day on the script,' recalls Harris. 'We pulled it into shape.'

Tension continued to bedevil *Mutiny on the Bounty*. Milestone gave up in despair and was replaced by George Seaton, a capable but undistinguished studio director. The picture closed down for several months while everyone tried to decide on the ultimate ending.

Harris and Elizabeth returned to Los Angeles. He was glad to distance himself from the rows and arguments of *Mutiny*. Later, he was recalled to Hollywood to reshoot scenes in the movie. To avoid a repetition of the trouble with Brando, MGM arranged for Harris to say some of his lines not to Brando but to someone standing in for him out of camera.

It was an artful compromise, and though Harris found it unsatisfactory, he was left with no other option. 'The last scene of the picture, where Brando lies dying, I said my piece to a wooden box,' he recalled. 'That was my last scene. I took off my make-up and my costume and was going home. Then a voice called, "Mr Harris to camera, please," and I answered and found Brando on the set for the same scene. They wanted me to speak my lines to him off-camera.

'I picked up the box, slammed it down in front of Marlon and said, "You can talk to that. That's what I had to do." MGM thanked me for being so co-operative and they offered me a three-picture contract.'

Mutiny on the Bounty – and the way people had been talking about Harris and Brando – proved a huge headache for MGM. In fact Joseph R. Vogel, MGM president, issued a statement about the picture and Brando's part in it:

> In recent months a number of published stories concerning *Mutiny on the Bounty* have stressed its high production costs and have attributed the blame for this to Marlon Brando. This is gravely unfair. The costs were caused by delay in the arrival of the *Bounty*, fires, storms, bad weather, illness and the resignation of the original director, Sir Carol Reed.

Vogel also blamed 'clashes of temperament among director, producer, writer and principal players'. In the end, the final budget had doubled from around $10 million to beyond $18 million. It was argued later that both Harris and Howard failed to receive Oscar nominations for their roles because of outspoken comments about Brando; the argument does not hold much water.

Generally this remake of an old classic was regarded as a total disaster. True it was plagued with trouble from the outset, but mainly to blame was the lack of an inspired script, as well as Brando's lack of confidence in the prepared script.

'*Mutiny* should have been a howling success,' argued Noel Purcell. 'You see, it had everything going for it but personality clashes got in its way. Maybe', he added seriously, 'Marlon Brando was the wrong choice for Fletcher Christian.'

Harris did not contribute to the controversy about the film's failure, except to retail 'quotable stories' about his troubles with Brando. No matter how he tried, the *Mutiny* saga continued to live with him for years. In every press interview he was quizzed about his part in the location battles.

'Christ, I survived, that was the main thing,' he would say with a laugh.

He was now thinking of *This Sporting Life*, a movie that promised to give him new scope as an actor. He had already struck up a fine rapport with Lindsay Anderson, the director.

As far as he was concerned, the future again looked rosy.

9 *Machin – a dreadful giant*

Harris identified with Frank Machin, the hero of *This Sporting Life*.

Machin, a rugby league star, is inarticulate, ruthless, exuding an animal sexuality. He tries to master the widowed Mrs Hammond (Rachel Roberts) with his knockabout techniques, and when she protests at this degradation, he socks her on the jaw – the most ungallant counter-blow since Gable slapped Carole Lombard – and retires brooding to a slum.

Off-screen, Harris's image of a hellraiser persisted, though he was by no means inarticulate. He had by now joined the League of Hard Drinkers that included Robert Shaw, Peter O'Toole, Richard Burton and Trevor Howard, and it soon became difficult to distinguish between the gentle, romantic, compassionate and story-telling Irishman and the noisy, aggressive and sometimes violent individual. As ever, nothing came in the way of his career, even if at times his silly behaviour came dangerously close to disrupting it.

Sex, he realized, was going to be the powerful underlying force in *This Sporting Life*, greater perhaps than was the case in *Room at the Top* and *Saturday Night Sunday Morning*. As he studied the script, he saw that sexual dominance was Frank Machin's controlling weapon in his raw relationship with his mistress, Mrs Hammond. The prospect of playing these scenes with Rachel Roberts excited him.

Instinctively, he felt the film was an important one, not only because it afforded him emotional scope and the chance to be with a movie from the start, but because it reflected a traditional way of life in the north of England.

It came as no surprise when censor John Trevelyan expressed some concern after reading the screenplay. He prepared a list of 'cautions'. It was clear that the permissive tide had not yet begun 'to rip through society or film-making'. Yet the sex scenes were expected to present fewer problems than those in *Saturday Night and Sunday Morning*. Trevelyan also sensed a feeling of violence going through *This Sporting Life* which he felt was almost certain to surface in the finished movie.

For the early 1960s the language was deemed inordinately rough and sexually explicit; furthermore, some of the scenes between Machin and the landlady, as when he forces her to have sex with him, became the subject of 'a particularly solemn caveat'. As the censor advised, 'We would not want to see Machin moving his hands over Mrs Hammond, bearing down on her and lying on top of her, and we would not want what I imagine would be the visual described by the phrase, "Their bodies are suddenly in spasm".'

There was also a caution on nudity: 'There are scenes of men in showers and changing rooms. We do not want any censorable nudity and even full-length back-view shots should be few and discreet.'

Harris wasn't unduly worried. He felt that there was still ample scope to bring in a good movie. He was enthusiastic about the project and couldn't wait to get started. An avid rugby union fan since his Limerick days, he now began to involve himself totally in the league game and travelled north to watch teams like Wigan, Warrington and Leeds. The physical aspect of the game appealed to him and he liked watching the big matches which had plenty of 'needle' in them.

In a bid to get fully fit, he went into training to play the role of Frank Machin. He lived as an athlete, trained with dumbells and walked about the West End squeezing rubber exercisers in each palm. And for weeks he trained with Richmond rugby union team. As he recalled, 'I suppose I could have played with the London-Irish, but I thought that if I played with a toffee-nosed club I wouldn't be noticed. I wasn't. Nobody on the team spoke to me.'

The self-denying landlady was portrayed by the spirited Rachel Roberts. Tested for the part with four other actresses, director Lindsay Anderson decided she was ideal, though she protested, 'I'm too emotional … I'm too Welsh.' Anderson told her, 'I want all the emotions you have, but I want you to keep them bottled up inside you and make us feel the force that this woman uses to suppress all that's natural in life.'

He felt that Harris was a bit awed by Ms Roberts. As he said, 'You see, she lacked self-confidence until she began to act the part. Then she was totally secure in it. She could acquit herself with a first-rate reading in just a couple of takes. Richard took a few more to feel that he had got it right. Rachel's security as an actress made him feel respectful towards her.'

Once, when the director and Harris got locked in argument during rehearsals and ignored her, she said with exasperation, 'Look, when you bloody kids have finished, let me know.' She stormed off to her dressing-room and did not return. 'They're not going to treat the future Mrs Rex Harrison like this!' she said next day to producer Karel Reisz.

The late Colin Blakely had played a small part in *Saturday Night and Sunday Morning* but was still hoping for a worth-while film part. Cast as a friend of Frank Machin, he believed he had got the 'break' at last. 'I was greatly impressed by the storyline' he said at the time. 'It was meaty, the characterization was strong and the film seemed to be saying something.'

Lindsay Anderson's motto was, 'To make a film is to create a world,' and he was determined to create the 'muddy' world surrounding rugby league, on and off the pitch. From the beginning he had wanted Harris. More than once he recalled the circumstances of their first meeting. 'I flew out to Tahiti. The tears and tantrums everyone was going through were a godsend to us. Harris turned to *This Sporting Life* with relief and gratitude and his intuition that the book was so well-constructed that any departure from it would be to the film's detriment proved absolutely right.'

Anderson and his producer Karel Reisz agreed that David Storey should write the script, but Storey's first and second drafts for *This Sporting Life* were unacceptable. His third, however, proved satisfactory. After a few weeks of shooting, Anderson ran into problems and it looked as if he might be asked to resign. 'After four weeks they wanted to take me off the film,' he recalled. 'Harris was being obstinate.'

Anderson himself was also proving difficult and he was just as unwilling to compromise as was Harris, if he felt the rightness of his viewpoint. For example, Harris wanted the rugby scenes to be 'fierce and bloody', but Anderson warned him against 'going over the top'. The truth was that both director and actor were over-anxious, though this was only one of the reasons. 'It was an unhappy period,' remembered Colin Blakely, 'but we didn't want to see Lindsay go. It was *his* film as much as Richard Harris's. I think that he had some problem controlling the crew members and certain technical aspects seemed to puzzle him.'

'What probably saved him was his consummate assurance with players, in particular Harris and Rachel Roberts,' said one observer. 'For here Anderson fell back on traditional theatre methods of rehearsing them prior to shooting. This continued during the evenings of filming and over the weekends.'

Anderson, a painstaking director, continued to have some disagreements with Harris but they were not serious enough to delay the movie. The episode underlined another side of the actor – his determination to get things right as he saw them. Thoroughness, and professionalism, were the words he used when asked about his approach to filming. He did not want to let the big opportunity slip because of any weakness in the script or shoddy detail. Colin Blakely was impressed by Harris's single-minded approach.

'I was amazed. He had learned a lot in a short time. On the rugby field he looked like one of those big Wigan forwards capable of gobbling you up. He simply lived the role of Frank Machin. Really he couldn't miss with an approach like that.'

To Harris, the character of Frank Machin was completely authentic. In his travels up north he saw a hundred Frank Machins. He decided that 'Machin needs and loves this woman Mrs Hammond.' He found the end very touching, for when Machin has broken through the barrier of inarticulation, Mrs Hammond is dying in the county hospital and Machin's big fist is seen smashing a symbolic spider above her bed. It marks his beginning as a man, and also his end.

The première of *This Sporting Life* was scheduled for the Odeon in Leicester Square in early February 1963. It was a black-tie affair and Harris had invited scores of friends, including Tom Stack from Limerick, and Ireland's best-known show-business columnist, Des Hickey.

'He might justifiably have shown a celebrity's disdain at the black-tie première,' says Hickey, 'but he was as excited as a schoolboy. I am happy to report that he remains native, rude, blunt and loyal.'

It was true. Harris never forgot his *real* friends. The atmosphere 'throbbed with adulation'. Among the first-nighters were Albert Finney and Tom Courtenay. 'Richard, you were enormous,' said Courtenay. In London his friends called him Richard; in Limerick he was still Dickie Harris.

Outside the cinema, crowds waited hopefully in the rain for a brief glimpse of the new idol before a studio limousine would whisk him away. Suddenly they were astonished when the star stood bare-headed on the pavement, wearing over his dinner jacket an astrakhan-collared topcoat that seemed to have come from Richard Burton's wardrobe, calling greetings to friends and relatives from Limerick. When at last he stepped into a car he was driven, not to the Savoy, but to the scene of his early struggles, the Troubadour, the cosy coffee bar where he was first introduced to his wife Elizabeth, and where he had auditioned her for a part in his West End production.

Forgetting *This Sporting Life* for a fleeting moment, he asked Hickey to follow him downstairs to a cellar where he had once been allowed to bed down when he hadn't the price for 'digs' or a room.

'That's the very spot,' Harris said, pointing to a corner in the basement where two friendly-looking regulars were uncapping bottles of beer.

The actor and his wife Elizabeth had invited to the wine and punch party those who had believed in the actor before he reached stardom. There were no outsiders. And at the bar was a cake shaped like a rugby pitch with tiers of chocolate seats and a marzipan player about to kick a chocolate ball. Producer Karel Reisz cut the cake by stabbing at the marzipan with a knife.

There were familiar faces at the tables. Lindsay Anderson chatted with novelist David Storey, while J.P. Donleavy found a place to sit, after some difficulty. 'It was a real celebratory atmosphere in the candlelit room,' recalls Tom Stack. 'I think everyone was aware that the film was a success and was a turning point for Richard.'

Lindsay Anderson was too shy to make a speech. But Harris said, 'Thank you for coming, my friends. I hope you may go back to see *Sporting Life*. I see Donleavy is here tonight. I want to film *The Ginger Man*, with Lindsay directing. Then *Wuthering Heights*. I had planned to play *Hamlet* at the Edinburgh Festival, but now Peter O'Toole is going to do it with Olivier as Claudius.'

In Hickey's view Harris realized that *Sporting Life* had gained him star status. He would henceforth be able to command £200,000 a picture. 'I suppose it's inevitable that I will make another Hollywood movie,' he said. 'But I'll agree to no picture unless the part is right.'

The meaning of fame was quickly brought home to him. 'Everybody wants to speak to me,' he said. 'I have had to change my pub and have scratched my name from the residents' board in the vestibule of my flat.' 'If not the best,' London critic Robert Vas commented on the film, 'it is certainly the rudest, roughest and most ruthless.'

Dilys Powell, the *Sunday Times* reviewer went to see *This Sporting Life* twice. She considered it 'an important film, and capable of standing on its own'. It brought back a name that had been missing too long from the screen, Lindsay Anderson.

To Miss Powell, everything in the film had its bearing on the nature and the actions of the man and woman (Harris and Rachel Roberts) and their treatment of one another: the violence and tenacity and arrogance of the man, the rebellion and resentment, softened for no more than a scene or two, of the woman.

The Man in Richard Harris's splendid fierce lowering portrait, regards life as an act of defiance. You see him, when emotional generosity is demanded of him, folding his arms in a skinflint gesture; he can never, until it is too late, admit dependence on anybody. He is destroyed by his own fault. He is a tragic hero.

While Harris was pleased with his own performance, and the film itself was regarded as a splendid artistic success, there were reservations expressed about its commercial drawing power by, among others, Lindsay Anderson and producer Karel Reisz, who observed sadly, 'There was a ruthless quality about it ... rightly charmless in the acting ... But people came away having been pained rather than cheered.'

Critic Alexander Walker wrote:

It didn't help its commercial chances to be represented in some quarters as the story of a footballer, since exhibitors told Anderson that sporting stories were box-office disasters before they got screened.

The reason for the 'chill reception', Anderson believed, was due to something deeper and more complex about the film and had to do with the central character Frank Machin and his relationship with Mrs Hammond. As he said, 'It was an intimidating subject for a film.'

Later, however, Harris was named Best Actor of the year at the Cannes Film Festival for his performance. He won the vote against such competition as Gregory Peck, whose acting in *To Kill a Mocking Bird* won him a Hollywood Oscar.

Harris was not in Cannes when the award was announced. After watching the showing of the film on Sunday he flew home to London to be with Elizabeth as she gave birth to their third son. They decided to call him Jamie.

The actor showed his compassionate side shortly afterwards when, unreported, he gave a large sum of money earned from *Sporting Life* to Rank Flour Mills, who had taken over his father's mill in Limerick, to prevent their closing it down. Economically, it was a futile gesture, since Rank closed the mill the day after the old man's death, but it was important to Harris. 'I didn't want my father to die thinking he was a failure.'

Elizabeth Harris had firm views about Lindsay Anderson. 'He became one of Richard's best friends,' she said. 'He was loyal, possessive, erudite, and his taste and knowledge encouraged a new dimension within my husband. They would fight and argue, yet Richard was always impressed by Lindsay's intellectual brawn.'

Harris saw Anderson as a kind of lucky omen. They teamed up again in March 1963 to present *The Diary of a Madman* at the Royal Court Theatre, having adapted the stage version from a Gogol short story. The story is about a government clerk in St Petersburg who lives in a bed-sitting room and has a fantasy world which he finally enters.

'Lindsay and I have been working on this for three months,' announced Harris. 'I took the play to a psychiatrist and we had a chat, and he said it was a perfect picture of a schizophrenic. Very powerful stuff.'

There was a new confidence about the actor, a new urgency to express himself. As he said, 'I feel I have something to say in life, something to contribute. You see, acting is not my passion. I wouldn't bet you that in two years I'd still be acting. I could be doing anything. None of my family were actors. Perhaps I'll do a musical. That would appeal to me.'

To show-biz columnists, he was a puzzle, a compulsive talker who embellished stories and understandably they did not accept all the blarney they heard from the ebullient Irishman. In their eyes, his latest Gogol venture was a 'piece of self-indulgence', to which Harris replied, 'I wanted to do something heroic, something that is grand theatre.'

'Mr Harris has a small boy's total absorption in that which he is doing at the moment,' commented one reporter, somewhat cynically. The actor observed, '*This Sporting Life* is dead – *The Diary of a Madman* is alive.'

To the majority of the critics, the Gogol work did not actually come alive on stage. They were disappointed with the result of the Harris–Anderson labours. 'It will probably prove to be the most tedious theatrical entertainment of the season,' observed the critic Herbert Kretzmer under the heading: 'A MAD NIGHT OUT IN SLOANE SQUARE'.

And of the actor's performance, he stated:

Mr. Harris, of course, is a fine and muscular and intelligent actor and he rages splendidly in his cellar room, crawling like a dog, imagining himself on the throne of Spain, confiding his dreams of personal glory in his diary. But even a virtuoso role such as this needs a coherent line of development, progress, direction, purpose. One leaves the theatre feeling that one has seen a celebrated actor at a party having engaged in a piece of self-indulgence and having gone at it too long.

Soon, Harris would be leaving behind his 'schizophrenic world' and taking the plane to Rome to begin work on an Antonioni film, *The Red Desert* (Il Deserto Rosso). Since his acclaim in *This Sporting Life* film offers were pouring in and the stage would have to wait. He looked forward to working with the celebrated, if enigmatic, director.

10   Heston's 'lordly manner'

Filming *The Red Desert* was, on his own admission, an unhappy experience, if not a downright frustrating one. Since he spoke no Italian, and Antonioni had few words of English, communication was almost impossible. Furthermore, Harris was puzzled by the director's habit of occasionally choosing new cast members from the streets of Rome. It seemed he liked amateurs better than professionals. 'He's a genius, but mad,' summed up Harris.

However, his frustration during this period was eased somewhat when he was approached by Columbia to play a starring role in *Major Dundee*, a story based on the American Civil War and which explored the conflict between the two major characters, both Southerners, one a loyal officer, the other a Confederate.

Charlton Heston, the star of the film, also had a say in the casting. He and the then-unknown director Sam Peckinpah had both seen a run-through of *This Sporting Life* and were impressed by Harris's compelling performance and agreed that he was right for the role of Tyreen. Columbia had sought Anthony Quinn, and also considered Steve McQueen, but Quinn was unavailable and McQueen was not interested.

In Rome, Harris read the script and was enthusiastic. Columbia's fee was, in his agent's view, inadequate and the film company was asked to increase it. In a bid to talk Harris into accepting, producer Jerry Bressler flew to Rome from Los Angeles for discussions and after what looked like stalemate finally Harris agreed. 'I'm satisfied,' he said. 'I'll do it.'

'We must not compromise on the casting,' Heston told director Sam Peckinpah, who was getting impatient with delays in starting the film. He was annoyed with Michelangelo Antonioni who refused to release Harris because, he claimed, *The Red Desert* was behind schedule.

Harris had grown weary of the Italian director's ponderous direction and his personal treatment of Monica Vitti. 'Antonioni controls her life,' he said. There was also a communication problem. The director did not speak any English, so their conversations were 'limited to mime and gestures open to numerous interpretations'. Harris summed up, 'He's a genius, but I don't understand the man.'

Eventually, he joined the *Major Dundee* cast and crew in Mexico. He admitted he was tired after his lengthy Rome experience. Heston, meanwhile, was unhappy with the script. 'If we can't get it right after five and a half months in the typewriter, then we have to get it right in front of the cameras.' He regretted that Harris had been delayed, for as he pointed out to Peckinpah, 'I wish they'd released him earlier; we could have used some of the time working together on the script.'

The film posed an exciting new challenge for Harris. Although years before his father had ridden with the hunt in County Limerick he himself had only a limited knowledge of horses. But Heston recalled, 'We checked out the cast in the saddle. Only James Coburn can horseback. Dick Harris looks loose on a horse, which is a plus. The others will get by, I expect.'

Heston, who persisted in calling Harris by the name Dick, was his complete opposite. Where Harris had a sense of the absurd and was fun-loving and irreverent, Heston possessed a bigger ego, was a disciplinarian and, like Brando, wanted, it appeared, to take over every film he was doing. This was to lead to conflict with Peckinpah.

To the outgoing Harris, Heston was simply 'a square', and he elaborated, 'I'm against the "squares" of this world because they're afraid of having their corners cut off.' What he principally had against the star was his lordly manner on the set 'as if he was the whole goddam production, instead of just an actor'.

Heston would arrive early, precisely on time, and glance with pursed lips at the tousled arrival of Harris. So Harris went out and bought an alarm clock, and strung it around his neck. He appeared in the studio the next day before Heston, and timed the alarm so that it shrieked off when the other arrived on the set. They didn't speak afterwards, but Harris didn't mind; he'd struck his blow for doing his own thing.

There is an old adage in rugby that the bigger they come the harder they fall, and it was something Harris liked to practise, especially when he met them in the film world. He was always careful, though, to keep within the realms of professionalism. When Peckinpah suggested, for instance, that he play his role in an Irish accent, he did not disagree. Heston remarked, 'We'll make him an honest Irishman. Lots of Irishmen fought in our Civil War.'

To Harris, Peckinpah had both flair and imagination. But with the film running over budget and over schedule there was a danger that the director would get the sack. He was not particularly liked by the Columbia top brass and producer Jerry Bressler regarded him as 'difficult to manage'. The company had by now moved location to Mexico City. The four weeks in Durango had seemed an eternity to some of the crew and cast.

Off-screen, Harris avoided Heston and preferred instead the genial company of James Coburn, an actor as he said 'after my own heart'. Together they went to bullfights at the Plaza de Toros, and at the climax of the spectacle Harris would jump to his feet with excitement. With his wife Elizabeth joining him in Mexico, he seemed more relaxed and less moody.

They moved out to the village for more location shots – a new experience for Harris. It was April and the sun was hot, the climate reminiscent of Spain. 'Christ only knows how I picked up a cold in this heat,' lamented Heston. Came the final battle scene with the French: Heston accused Harris of using the wrong rifles in two important shots, which had to be repeated after lunch, costing them an hour and a half's shooting light.

Tempers became frayed. Peckinpah attributed the tensions to Columbia's ultimatum to finish the film within schedule. Heston admitted that he had been unfair to Harris and blamed his own anger on the gruelling location. Harris, who had picked up a good deal of knowledge about horses and less about guns, reckoned Peckinpah was doing a good job. His attitude towards Heston hadn't changed. He summed up the actor as 'having issued from a cubic womb'. It was a description that would travel round the world.

It was May, and Peckinpah had survived the film. No one, it appeared, had dared purge him. 'It would have been an absolutely lousy idea,' said Heston. 'Aside from Sam's talent, you don't change horses, if you can help it, in mid-stream. I am

positive the picture's only chance lies in Sam's finishing it. I told
Jerry Bressler as much.'

Harris grew a beard for his next role of Cain in *The Bible*. He
welcomed the opportunity of working with John Huston, a
director he had long admired. It was his first biblical role and the
cast included Peter O'Toole as the three angels(!) and George C.
Scott as Abraham, whose off-screen love for Ava Gardner
provided a field day for the gossip columnists.

Huston revealed that *The Bible* was the most extensive thing
he had ever undertaken. To Harris, he epitomized the acme of
professionalism and before he left Italy he told the veteran
director that he'd like to work for him again. Huston, for his
part, summed up the Irish actor as 'ebullient' but no saint in the
biblical sense.

Back in London, Harris spent his money freely and gathered
more friends around him. Some of his escapades with the
rumbustious Irishman Malachy McCourt found their way into
the English Sunday papers, and left both men with monumental
hangovers. On his return from Rome, Harris decided to
celebrate with a late-night party. However, neighbours in quiet
Bedford Gardens, Kensington bitterly complained about the
appalling noise.

Predictably, the actor hit back. He paid a man to walk up and
down the street carrying sandwich boards reading: 'LOVE THY
NEIGHBOUR HARRIS'. The man also rang a bell to draw
attention to the notice. 'I'm hoping Mr Harris will pay me
danger money,' he said. But all that happened as he paraded up
and down with his appeal were a few shouts from neighbours of
'Go back to Stratford, Harris.'

Harris, who never cared much what people thought about
him, declared, 'I don't care what the neighbours say. Sure I had
a party. And if I want to give another I will.' Eight neighbours
called at the house to protest after the party ended at 5 a.m.

Elizabeth Harris and her children slept soundly through the
noisy revelries. At times, she had to admit that life with Richard
was becoming more intolerable. Fame wasn't making him any
more responsible; if anything he was determined to live up to
his popular image as a hellraiser. Alcohol made his temper

worse and when he became belligerent he'd throw furniture around or get into scrapes in pubs or restaurants. Paradoxically, he could be fun-loving and serious as he talked endlessly about movies, particularly the ones he wanted to make. He still possessed enough pride in his work to make him seek new challenges.

Once he brought along Father Tom Stack to the cinema to see *The Red Desert* and became furious when he discovered that Antonioni had virtually edited him out of the film.

'Christ, he has turned me from a vertical to a horizontal man.'

Stack could see that his patience had been sorely tried. He listened as the actor talked of the total lack of understanding between him and Antonioni and how the latter kept them waiting for hours on the set as he worked out ingenious lighting and camera angles.

Major Dundee was another matter. 'Richard Harris showed dash and charm,' said Pauline Kael in the *New Yorker*. The critics were on the whole generous to him. In Heston's view, though, the movie was neither as bad as he feared nor as good as he hoped. As he said, 'The people are believable, the dialogue good, as are all the performances. However, the whole film is somewhat diffuse, and the story is as it always was, too complicated.'

Peckinpah complained that he hadn't been given a totally free hand, otherwise he would have made the film 'we all hoped for'. Heston doubted his words, and summed up, 'I think we all wanted to make a different sort of film. Columbia wanted a cowboy and Indians story, I wanted a film that dealt with the basic issues of the Civil War.' Harris, for his part, was not over-enthusiastic and later did not count *Major Dundee* as among his best film achievements.

In the middle of 1964, Elizabeth Harris confided in a friend: 'We have survived the hard times, and now we have the job of surviving success.'

It was true. They returned from Honolulu where Richard had been filming *Hawaii* and she noticed that his mood hadn't improved. As she said, 'I felt more than ever that we were being irrevocably forced apart by emotional chaos and a paranoia I didn't understand. My own grip on any emotion except fear was tentative.'

When he got into fights, there was nothing she could do. What should have been the most marvellous time of their lives, she reflected, had become a nightmare. 'We had three healthy children. Richard had success and fame. We had money. My only thoughts now were keeping out of his way.'

Nonetheless, they continued to enjoy some marriage 'highs' and dined out or went party-going. Harris could be the most convivial of company and on such occasions tended to forget domestic quarrels. Suddenly, he might say, 'Let's go out, Liz.' It was as simple as that. She would dress and set out hoping for a blissful evening, but she was also prepared for the worst. By now she had no illusions.

On one occasion, they went out together to the Mirabelle restaurant in Curzon Street, Mayfair, where they joined David Newman, the burly film producer. After a while the talk came round to politics and the producer said he didn't want to talk about the subject as he considered that all politicians were a lot of jokers.

Harris objected to what he said and to everyone's dismay both men went outside. In the street Harris's friends tried to separate them, but blows were exchanged and the actor fell to the ground. Picking himself up he went back inside to rejoin Newman at his table. The producer announced, 'The fight is over.' He said he had known Richard Harris for a long time, and they were friends. The actor's thumb was badly bruised.

The incident illustrated Harris's short fuse and impetuosity. Friends advised him to slow down on his drinking, fearing that he would kill himself. The self-destructive forces in him were by now becoming more obvious. If he was not careful, the one thing he cherished above all else – his career – would be damaged.

Typically, he made light of public incidents. He laughed as he brandished his bruised thumb and explained, 'I got that hitting David Newman. As he came at me I stepped aside and handed him off rugby style – with my fist. He went down with a thud and I had to take him to the wash room to look after him.'

Sometimes Elizabeth was drawn inadvertently into his rows. But on this occasion she sided with her husband. 'This time Richard was right. Newman says my father's name was not mentioned – it's utterly untrue.'

Since the 1960s were associated with the hellraising days in the business, no one became alarmed by the activities of The League of Hard Drinkers, nor took them too seriously. It was a facet of show-business, nothing more. It was noticeable, though, that the hellraisers were more associated with the screen than the stage. One actor remarked, 'Really it's a matter of money. Screen stars have more to spend.'

Harris had no time to think about the public's attitude. He was off to Rome to film *Three Faces of a Woman*. His co-star? Princess Soraya.

11 'Soraya's a beautiful gimmick'

'Soya.' It seemed no way to address Princess Soraya, the former Queen of Persia and now his co-star in *Three Faces of a Woman*. But it showed Harris's contempt once more for conformity.

He had no intention of paying court to the princess. As he explained, 'I don't pander to anyone, not even my father-in-law, Lord Ogmore.'

Off-screen, a certain protocol was to be observed, with everyone expected to go to her table before going to their own. 'I wouldn't have it,' recalled Harris. 'I decided to either treat her as a princess or as an actress. You can't have it both ways. I was the only person treating her sincerely, you see.'

Relations between them were cool for a while. Princess Soraya made it clear that she considered the actor 'rude'. He had had a brush with one of her entourage over how to pronounce her name. He called her Soya. However, he considered her as beautiful on screen as Sophia Loren.

It was a surprise when he accepted the role in the film. A few stars had already said no. And since he had recently refused a Hollywood offer of £100,000 to act in *The Fall of the Roman Empire*, the only logical reason for his decision was that he wouldn't return to Hollywood unless it was a plum role. After his humiliating experience there in *The Wreck of the Mary Deare*, he naturally wanted to return in triumph.

Anyway, he did not need the money urgently. He admitted he had got 'a tidy bit tucked away'. After there was a delay in payment of his fee for *Three Faces of a Woman* he went on record as saying that making films 'without the dough is a dead loss'.

From the outset, he was worried about the script. 'Unless I get a better script I'm walking out,' he told the Italian producers. He explained that he had accepted the role in the first place because the storyline was marvellous, but when he read the finished script he thought it was ghastly.

Second time around it was more acceptable to him. He felt that if Princess Soraya flopped in the film she could say goodbye to a screen career. 'I think she has the basic quality that made Grace Kelly a star,' he predicted.

During shooting in Rome, he lived up to the lifestyle of a star. Lean and red-bearded, he was photographed with Princess Soraya, and in the evenings went to the best restaurants. On other occasions, he received Fleet Street columnists in his hotel suite and talked endlessly about film projects. The theatre seemed miles away.

Once, in the late afternoon, he treated Roderick Mann of the *Sunday Express* to champagne and swore he had given up brandy, whisky and vodka for the time being. He had come to the door of his Rome hotel suite, barefoot and crumpled, as though he had been asleep. He was wearing a blue denim shirt and black trousers pulled up below his knees, fisherfolk style.

As he perched himself on the corner of the settee, his legs tucked under his chin, he sipped his glass of champagne and said reflectively, 'They all think this movie is going to be bloody awful, but it won't. It's marvellous, despite everything.' Clearly, he was making no apologies for accepting the role, though he did not need to be reminded that other stars refused because as an actress Princess Soraya was regarded as a novice.

He got up and paced about the room. As ever, he wanted an audience. 'Look at me,' he said casually. 'I am a tramp. I don't care about clothes, you see. My wife Liz has found this man who has exactly the same measurements as myself. When my clothes begin to fall off me she just has this man measured for a new suit and brings it home to me ready-made. She is a great girl, Liz. Her job is to keep me alive and she does it well.'

The Harrises may have had their quarrels at home and marriage at times seemed more like a war, but the actor was not above lauding Elizabeth to the world. Regularly she came into his conversation, so did the children, and he assured all and sundry that he was a family man.

This afternoon in his suite he persisted in looking back on his early days – perhaps because it was his birthday: he was thirty-two. 'When we got married everyone was against it,' he said, after another sip of champagne. 'She was Lord Ogmore's daughter and they didn't want her marrying some ugly Irish actor from the bogs, and my people didn't want me, a good

Roman Catholic, marrying a Protestant. So we got no presents. Nothing at all. We started out in life eight years ago with nothing but a four-poster bed and a large tin trunk. Green it was.'

He handed out more champagne. He was sober, yet his preoccupation with the past was extremely puzzling. Rome, with its memories, might have provided more readable copy. But he persisted. 'I am a Socialist, and my father-in-law's a Liberal, and I won't have him in the house. I told him to go. I told him his presence was a continual source of embarrassment to me because of his politics. I also told him the House of Lords was nothing but a rich man's Labour Exchange, where a lot of old men signed on each day and drew their money.'

The phone rang once. Twice. Three times. He answered it first as an Indian, next as a German. Then as a Korean. It was convincing. No one hung up. The actor's mood brightened as he poured more champagne, and said, 'I drink this as wine.'

In a café later he grew more nostalgic and burst into song and for a moment accompanied the guitarist. Life again was a celebration. It was very late by the time he returned to his suite.

Back in London, he was acquiring the status symbols that go with stardom. In his house in Bedford Gardens he had filled the shelves with books, hung more valuable pictures on the walls, and bought records by the score. He even bought himself a Rolls-Royce and hired a chauffeur.

When his Limerick friends flew into Heathrow, he would say to the chauffeur, 'Collins, fetch my friends from the airport.' Soon the Rolls became known as the 'Limerick Special'. Once, when Collins was driving Father Tom Stack from the airport, the priest felt slightly embarrassed, but chuckled when Collins remarked, 'If they see you sitting there, Father, you'll get nothing for the church collection next Sunday.'

Stack found there was an inquisitive side to the actor. 'Dickie loved going around unusual places in London, like quaint shops and libraries and historic buildings. It was a side of his character that few knew about. On these little adventures I found him entertaining and excellent company. Needless to say he wouldn't be drinking.'

After the success of *This Sporting Life* some Irish actors in

London accused Harris of putting on 'airs and graces'. Malachy McCourt laughed and said that Dickie Harris would never change, not for the devil himself.

It wasn't quite true. Harris knew he was a star and never tried to disguise it. He moved easily among stars. Friends wondered whether Elizabeth could tolerate the *new* Richard Harris that threatened to engulf her. She saw herself as an equal, as a partner in their relationship, not solely as a supportive wife.

Yet, she admitted she was beginning to feel 'suffocated'. As she explained, 'The house was bursting with Richard. People came to talk to Richard. People telephoned Richard. People discussed Richard and listened to Richard. The house was organized for Richard. Richard was fond of telling people that my sole job was to keep him alive.'

That the *Three Faces of a Woman* proved pretty disastrous did not worry Harris. He did not try to unload the blame on to ex-Queen Soraya. He described her as a beautiful gimmick and thought there was an interesting aloofness about her. Yet he passionately defended the Princess against criticism.

Aware of the criticism levelled at him for doing the movie, he countered by saying that he had plans to balance his career. 'I'll do an artistic film and then a boy's adventure story,' he said.

At times, he liked to talk about the films he had made, as if to answer any criticisms. In every interview he gave he was asked about *This Sporting Life* and was annoyed if anyone argued that it was a failure.

'That is an ungenerous thing to say,' he replied firmly. 'The film did have a down-beat atmosphere; perhaps I was not well-known enough to carry full weight from a box-office point of view. But I don't look at it as a failure. We set out to achieve something; we set a standard and reached it. It was only a failure to the shareholders.'

When he was asked about Marlon Brando, he was also forthcoming: 'He is difficult and boring. He doesn't play a scene with you – everything's secret. He doesn't pour on the coal in the first take, but lets it go on to the eleventh and suddenly it clicks for him. "That's it," he says and walks off. Meanwhile your best take may have been number three. It's a self-centred sort of art. Brando has a great talent – it's electrifying. But he's lost his way.' He was working hard to expunge the memories of *Mutiny on the Bounty*, a very unhappy picture as far as he was concerned.

Hawaii, even more spectacular but a good period picture, was to erase all that. The character of Rafer Hoxworth fascinated him.

'I like him because of his tremendous conceit. Imagine a chap taking off after saying to the girl he loved, "I'll see you in two years," and coming back as promised, not a day earlier, expecting her to be there, waiting.

'And she's gone, naturally. Then a couple of years later he meets her in Hawaii, and he says, "Why didn't you wait for me?" She says, "Well, you didn't write!" And he, "I wrote you four times!" Mind you, four times in two years. And she says, "Anyway, I can't go away with you. I'm married and I'm having a baby." So he says, "Okay, you have your baby, then I'm coming back and taking you off the island." And he comes back, all of five years later and truly expects her to leave her husband and to come with him.

'And somehow I admire that. The tremendous enormity that is life, embraced and lived in this style. Live to the fullest, because you only have it once.'

His next movie, *The Heroes of Telemark* took him to Norway and the Rjukan Valley – to co-star with Kirk Douglas who was cast as Doctor Rolf Pederson, a Norwegian scientist reluctant to join Harris and the underground against the Nazis.

The two actors were described as 'volatile' and it was claimed by the press that when they met for the first time in a Los Angeles hotel, prior to departure for Norway, they regarded one another warily. Harris never cared for abrasive Hollywood stars. He remained suspicious not only of colleagues in the business, but of people generally.

However, in the hotel lounge, Douglas called across the floor, 'Don't believe a word of it.'

Harris climbed to his feet and jokingly clenched his fists. 'Hold it, Kirk!' he shouted. 'Do you want it now, or shall we step across the river into Texas?' Everybody laughed. It was the kind of lighthearted scene that broke the ice at the start of the movie. At first there was some dispute about who should get the close-ups, but this soon evaporated. When Harris arrived in Rjukan the sun was shining on the snow-laden slopes and all was well with the 100-plus location team, headed by director Anthony Mann.

Ironically, Mann had been fired by Douglas on *Spartacus* but the actor unhesitatingly accepted the director's offer to play Dr Pederson. 'It was exciting to make the movie,' says Douglas, 'because it was based on the true story of a heavy-water plant in Norway that was crucial to the Nazis.'

Harris was to say that in *The Heroes of Telemark* he played the part rather than lived it. They were dogged by rough weather, but he considered the filming 'a piece of cake'. It wasn't as simple as that. There were scenes where he and Douglas had to hang over a gorge, three hundred feet from the ground. 'All I needed was confidence,' he recalled. 'I pretended it was only two feet high and that I'd fall into a bed.'

He admitted that when location work began, he and Kirk Douglas trod warily. Both were single-minded, tough, and no-nonsense guys; however, before long they knew exactly where they stood with each other. 'It wasn't long before we hit it off,' Harris says. What pleased him was that the movie was shot where it really happened, in a small town in the valley near Rjukan, north of Oslo, and the film used Norwegians who had been involved in the event.

Like Douglas, he was glad that they did the picture with Anthony Mann, for it was the last complete picture he directed. He was in the middle of *A Dandy in Aspic* with Laurence Harvey when he died.

It was noticeable by now that Harris was acquiring a smooth professional approach to each movie he did. He exuded confidence and was prepared to tackle the most awkward scenes. It made him feel good.

He wanted to be seen as a versatile actor. He signed a contract to do an entirely different kind of role opposite Doris Day in *Caprice*. He was returning to Hollywood and looked forward to the experience. *This Sporting Life* was opening new doors to him.

What he didn't know was that *Caprice* very nearly came unstuck even before he set out for America. When Doris Day was handed the script by the producer, she shook her head and protested, 'I read this script – all I can say is, thank God I don't have to make movies like that any more.'

'What are you talking about?'

Miss Day was adamant. 'You can't be serious – that's a terrible script.'

'You're wrong, Doris, and you'll realize it when you see how it turns out. Now I'll tell you who we've got – Richard Harris and —'

Before the producer could go on, she said, 'What are you trying to tell me?'

'That you have to make this picture.'

Although she was virtually forced to do it for 20th Century-Fox, she was unhappy because she felt it was a backward step for her after the successes of the early Sixties when she co-starred with Rock Hudson and James Garner in top-rated comedies.

Harris was quickly made aware that his co-star was unhappy with the script, but she seemed to have no intention of taking out her frustration on him. She got round the problem another way. As he explained, 'Doris simply switched the parts to suit herself. I finished up playing her part. And she played mine. After reading the script, she said, "I want Richard's role." So I said alright. So they changed the name Patricia to Pat and Christopher to Christina, and we swopped the roles.'

She had first seen the actor in *This Sporting Life*. Lindsay Anderson had surrounded Harris with little people in the movie to make him appear huge. His hair had been dyed very dark, he used dark make-up and his eyes were dark and sunken, to give him a brooding look. Miss Day discussed Harris with her husband, the producer Marty Melcher, who assured her that the actor was right for *Caprice*.

Later, when he arrived for a make-up test with the actress, she wasn't there. He waited an hour or two but there was no sign of her. After a few days, the film company got embarrassed bringing him in so they wheeled in a little dummy with a blond wig and clothes.

'I said "look here, I don't believe Doris exists," ' he recalls. 'I said, "I believe she's dead. She does not exist. Now I'm going home and tomorrow, if she is alive, bring her in and we'll meet." They apologized, and said Doris would come in the next day.'

Doris Day considered *Caprice* a bad investment for 20th Century-Fox and a bad movie, ranking it beside *Do Not Disturb*, *Ballad of Josie* and *Where Were You When the Lights Went Out?* As she said, 'There were good actors like Rod Taylor, Richard Harris and Peter Graves cast in them, but these poor men were the pearls before the swine of these scripts.'

Nor did Richard Harris rate it among his best movies. Once, when interviewed about it, he remarked, 'Somebody once asked what is the most dangerous thing you ever did and I said kissing Doris Day ...'

He also had another more traumatic reason for remembering *Caprice*. One day he collapsed on the soundstage and was taken to hospital by ambulance, thinking he was dying. He admitted he had lived in fear of death and at the time became convinced that he had a heart condition. The symptoms that day were familiar – a pain in his chest and arms.

'I'm losing my mind,' he told Dr Kennamer from Cedars of Lebanon hospital. 'Something is the matter. I'm drinking because of it. You must find out what's wrong. Once and for all ...'

Dr Kennamer assured him he would be kept in the hospital until they found out what was wrong. 'Take it easy, Mr Harris,' he advised him. A few days later his trouble was diagnosed as a scarred esophagus. The inflammation of his gullet had been brought about by the emotional tension he had been under for years. It was curable as long as he behaved sensibly, which meant easing up on the liquor.

Despite his dread of death, he said he felt pretty healthy. From Cedars of Lebanon Hospital, he returned to the magnificent mansion he had rented, one of the most beautiful estates in Hollywood, with its swimming pool and tennis courts and ballroom, and seventeenth-century ceilings brought over from Italy, and costly paintings on the walls. From where it stood on top of a private hill in Bel Air, it offered a commanding view of the city, and of the Pacific Ocean to the right.

He had a Mexican housekeeper, Lupe, and her husband Edgardo to take care of the grounds. Lupe was a good cook and in the evenings cooked some delicious meals for the actor. For Harris, gregarious by nature, it was a strange experience to be alone in such a large mansion. With his marriage in crisis, it looked like there would be more lonely days.

12 King Arthur's crown

Back in London he had decided he wanted to wear King Arthur's crown in *Camelot*.

It soon became an absolute obsession with him. Richard Burton had created the stage role on Broadway, and in London Laurence Harvey, as King Arthur, enjoyed a huge success in Drury Lane. It was no secret in the business that Harvey wanted the film part; he considered it his since Moss Hart had given him T.H. White's book, *The Once and Future King* which inspired the musical.

Joshua Logan, who would direct the film, said he had seen nothing in any of Harris's performances to indicate he could play the part. The actor did not accept such a dismissive view, and mounted a determined campaign. Every day from his house in Kensington he sent a different telegram to Logan pleading his case: 'ONLY HARRIS FOR ARTHUR'. 'HARRIS BETTER THAN BURTON'.

None generated a reply. A few hours after Logan arrived in London to begin casting, Harris burst into his suite at Claridges demanding a test.

'Look,' Logan replied categorically, 'I don't want you.'

That evening Logan and his wife went to a cocktail party. The waiter who came up to them with a tray of drinks was Harris. Logan shook his head incredulously.

'Jesus,' he exclaimed, 'will you leave me alone?'

'Never,' Harris arrogantly assured him. 'Wherever you go, I'll be there. If you go to the toilet, I'll pop out of the bowl. If you take a taxi, I'll jump in. If you catch a plane, I'll be in the next seat. All you have to do is test me.'

Logan finally relented – he probably had no other option. It came about when Harris nailed him in the hotel and offered to pay for his own screen test. Harris wasn't exactly confident about his own singing voice. As he said, 'I'd only ever sang in a boozer, and I'd thought I'd had it. But Logan saw what I felt and gave me the part.'

Today, the actor finds it hard to explain why he wanted the role so badly. 'It was a challenge, certainly,' he reflected, 'but more than that *Camelot* got under my skin. The soliloquy when Arthur recognizes the betrayal of Lance and Jenny, yet forgives them, never fails to move me. Could it possibly be civilized to destroy what I love?'

In turn, Burton and Harvey had previously been tipped for the film role of the king. Harvey had become friendly with the Harrises, but the friendship waned after he lost the role of King Arthur to the Irish actor. When he heard that Joshua Logan had cast Harris for *Camelot* with Vanessa Redgrave as Queen Guinevere he dismissed them as 'dirty Richard Harris and that female impersonator'.

'Richard was overwhelmed with happiness and relief, when he finally got the part,' says Elizabeth Harris. 'He felt it was a new beginning.'

Despite his hellraising image, film directors saw a regal side to Harris. 'He has this curiously royal demeanour mixed with an earthy quality, a combination completely appropriate for Arthur,' commented one. 'He is absolutely right for the part,' conceded Joshua Logan when criticism began to be levelled at his choice of actor for the role. 'I think he has a very beautiful and exciting voice.'

It was a compliment, even though belated, that instilled new confidence in the star. In London, he knew, Laurence Harvey had been hotly tipped for the role but as far as he was concerned it was up for grabs. In Limerick they were not greatly surprised that he had persuaded Logan to let him play the king. In his school days he had played in college musicals, and later at singalongs in seaside hotels he was always in demand. To Harris, it was more than singing; he simply loved the story of *Camelot* and identified with the role of King Arthur.

Equally, the choice of Vanessa Redgrave for the glamorous role of Queen Guinevere caused some comment. She was probably as well known for her passionate devotion to causes like banning the bomb as for being an actress. She was in the news, however. Her latest film *Morgan* won the award at the Cannes Film Festival. Directors found a kind of 'translucent quality' about her stage appearances, an ability to transform herself not just physically but psychologically and emotionally.

Vanessa's friends were not surprised when she was cast in a starring role in *Camelot*; they regarded her as very versatile, although conceding that she was not a musical comedy star. When someone wrote, 'she had a delightfully low, husky voice' he wasn't referring to Miss Redgrave's singing voice.

Before she set out to join Harris for *Camelot*, she insisted on a house with a small swimming-pool – not for herself, but so that Natasha and Joely, her two little daughters, could learn to swim.

Elizabeth Harris, meanwhile, had refused to return to Hollywood to join her husband in his palatial mansion. 'I couldn't face going back to Los Angeles,' she explained. 'I knew that our marriage was over. I loved the Richard that had been – the poetic Richard, the wild Richard, the Richard who thought swizzle sticks were imitation flowers. I was afraid of the man Richard had become.'

It was soon obvious that Harris would have to work hard to get his share of publicity. Before long, Vanessa Redgrave had fallen in love with Franco Nero, one of the cast of *Camelot*. Papers were full of their fairy-tale romance and gradually the passionate affair threatened to put Queen Guinevere into the shade.

Harris's marital problems could not have been dragged across the world stage at a worse time. He was about to achieve one of his greatest film ambitions; he had returned to Hollywood in triumph; now he was faced with a court order refusing him permission to take his children to America. At a hearing in London, Mr Joseph Jackson, for Elizabeth Harris, said that

Mr Harris was a man of considerable talent and exceptional success in his profession. His wife alleges that her husband drank to excess and would then go berserk with whoever was in sight. Unfortunately, too, he is addicted to using foul language. Perhaps this is not the disgrace it was, but when there are children using four-letter Anglo-Saxon words the time has come, perhaps for a halt.

The court was further told that Mrs Harris did not want to rejoin her husband in America and believed that if she did, she would have difficulty in getting the children back. She also feared that if her husband came back and went on 'a drinking bout' anything might happen.

Mr Jackson said that a divorce petition by Mrs Harris had been filed that day.

Harris's own reaction was, to put it mildly, somewhat extraordinary. From his utterances it did not appear that he appreciated the gravity of the situation, or perhaps he never expected Elizabeth to seek a divorce. When he arrived on a hurried visit at Heathrow Airport, he said, 'I am absolutely shattered by this divorce action. I knew nothing at all about it until I arrived. I flew here intending to give my wife a pleasant surprise. She did not know I was coming. She did exactly the same thing two weeks ago. It is just one of our little games.'

Earlier he had said, 'I treated my wife like a flower always. I will be in trouble in Hollywood over this trip. I sneaked away from the film set. I was going to stay only thirty-six hours and then get straight back. And take my family with me.'

Later, when Elizabeth was granted custody of their three children, the judge at the Divorce Court declared, 'There are evidently serious controversies between this husband and his wife, the merits of which have not been explored before me.'

The court was told that Harris sought a reconciliation with his wife. The actor, who was in court, collapsed in a corridor after the hearing. He recovered after a few minutes and left the courtroom in a chauffeur-driven Rolls-Royce.

It dawned on him at last that Elizabeth really wanted a divorce. In the past he had tended to put domestic rows behind him and carry on as if nothing had happened. However, when the recriminations got worse and when friends failed to mend the couple's differences there seemed no course but separation. On one occasion, Harris accused his wife of being unfaithful; clearly it was turning out to be a messy affair. For Elizabeth, it appeared there was no turning back.

While he continued filming *Camelot* in Hollywood, she and the three children went on living in the once dignified red-brick house in Kensington which had had its respectability shaken when the Harrises moved in.

Back in Hollywood the gossip columnists concentrated on the love of Vanessa Redgrave for Franco Nero, and in the midst of the hottest romance of the year, Harris's domestic troubles seemed to pale into insignificance; in truth he was often lonely in his mansion overlooking the Pacific Ocean and longed for the company of his small sons, whom he loved and missed greatly.

As the mammoth musical dragged on at enormous cost to Warner Bros (Guinevere's wedding dress alone cost $12,000), Harris said that he was exhausted and pretty sick of the Hollywood scene. If he was offered a million dollars to start another film he couldn't do it because, he said, he was so 'dead beat'. Yet, despite everything, he felt an inner satisfaction, a personal fulfilment he had rarely, if ever, experienced before.

'I attribute it to my work on *Camelot*,' he revealed. 'I think I have done some terrific stuff in the film. It's some of my greatest although I'm fed up and tired of it all.' Although when he talked in his studio dressing-room he looked white-faced and tired, as a professional he had tried to put aside his personal marriage problems in his big scenes with Vanessa Redgrave, whom he had come to admire enormously, both as an actress and as a woman.

Joshua Logan, the director who had originally refused to consider Harris for the part of the king, was by now converted. 'I felt that I began life again working with Richard,' he said. 'If *Camelot* lives up to its regal appearance, he will be a major reason for its success.'

Harris surprised Hollywood by his sheer professionalism. At the studio, technicians lavished praise on the star as one of the most careful craftsmen they had ever met. This was noticeable during the complicated operation of dubbing, more technically referred to as looping – snippets of film are spliced together to circle repeatedly through a projector – a process in which actors re-record phrases that need improvements.

'You can change a whole performance while looping,' says Harris, who showed a perfectionist's approach in the musical. He spent a full hour dubbing the one word *Camelot*. The loop was repeated seventy-two times for those three syllables.

He admitted he was tired after six months of being a king, but still worked carefully on his press quotes:

You've got to run the length of your wildness, that's what I always say.

I have the rare honour of knocking over a double-decker bus with a small Ford.

Playing the tragic role of the idealist king was more than just new to me, it changed me inwardly.

Every wrinkle tells a tale. I wouldn't eliminate a single wrinkle for a thousand dollars.

There's nothing in my life that I regret. You don't grow through victories, rather through defeats. And knowledge is nothing unless you can pass it on.

I'm only going to play kings from now on.

He turned few, if any, journalists away. They found him shrewd, but irresistible, intelligent if unsubtle. Some did not know what to expect, and writer Joe Borgzinner described how Harris 'incessantly gambols about, incredibly agile, lumbering like an elephant with sandpapered toes amid jungles of eggshells'.

Despite the rigours of filming, he had attended a string of parties, some of them wild. He virtually tore the petals off The Daisy, the discothèque where moviedom liked to cavort. 'Harris's lust for life is insatiable,' wrote one experienced Hollywood columnist. 'He is one of the few ribald, boisterous souls left in the film world.'

He lavished money on his friends. Nearly everyone employed in the making of *Camelot*, including technicians, got an expensive silver token from Tiffany's.

In June 1967 he returned to London. He was delighted to be back. From the sideboard in the sitting-room of his Chesham Place flat he produced a crown, the crown he had worn as Arthur in *Camelot*.

'They rang me to say it was missing,' he joked. 'They wondered if I could help them to find it. I said, "If you do find it, let me know because I'd like to have it." That threw them off the scent.'

On the last day of work, he also commandeered the bike that the studio gave him to get around the lot. Everybody in the cast had one; his bore a fancy placard with old-English lettering, 'King Arthur'.

When the producer discovered that Harris was absconding with the bike, he telephoned the studio gate. With the bike wedged into the back seat of his car, Harris roared out, leaving a

Harris shows off his ball skills to David Webb (of Chelsea FC) and
Rodney Marsh (of Queens Park Rangers) at the private screening of
Bloomfield.

Harris's second wife, the former fashion model Ann Turkel, pictured on one of her visits to Ireland.

The newlyweds, in white jeans and satin jackets, *en route* to a Hollywood party.

In New York, 1974.

Harris, mounted, in the 1972 movie *A Man Called Horse*.

Phil Coulter, composer and bandleader, who toured British theatres with Harris for the actor's one-man music show.

Harris is greeted in style at the Gaiety Theatre, Dublin, for the first night of Shaw's *John Bull's Other Island*.

Richard Harris, Roger Moore, Richard Burton and Hardy Kruger (left to right) play hardened mercenaries in *The Wild Geese* (1977). The film was shot on tough and sweltering locations in the Northern Transvaal.

The two Richards (Burton is here pictured with his wife Suzy) went on the wagon during the filming of *The Wild Geese*.

Harris announces to the Dublin media details of a University Scholarship Scheme set up in memory of his late brother Dermot.

The star in reflective mood answers reporters' questions at a Dublin press conference.

In the foyer of the Berkeley Court Hotel in Dublin where his brother-in-law Jack Donnelly (beside him at reception) is assistant manager.

studio guard whistling and waving futilely. As soon as he got it to his Malibu Beach house he was pedalling down the sands and right into the surf.

He talked about *Camelot* and revealed that Rex Harrison had advised him to sing his songs live in the film, for that was the best way. But Warners wanted him to pre-record them. Jack Warner had said, 'Under no circumstances will I permit them to be sung live.'

Warner was thinking of the rising production costs, yet *Camelot* was already running into millions of dollars. Harris, up to his pranks, rang Warner. 'Harris here,' he said. 'I don't care what they say about you, Mr Warner, from now on I'll defend you. You're a great man. Thank you for letting me do the songs live.'

Warner could not refuse a request like that.

The première of *Camelot* fitted easily into the Swinging Sixties in London. Although as a musical it would scarcely surpass in popularity *The Sound of Music* or *My Fair Lady*, it demanded attention because of its mammoth cost and its stars, Richard Harris and Vanessa Redgrave. The première was arranged as a charity show and the guests of honour were Princess Margaret and Lord Snowden. Vanessa Redgrave and Franco Nero, who played Lancelot in the musical, missed the occasion. They were filming in Yugoslavia.

Harris, looking as though there was no hint of divorce in the air, wore a forest-green, silver-embroidered tunic-length kaftan, which made Princess Margaret remark, 'I'm glad I didn't wear my kaftan – we might have clashed.'

But the actor's hippie gear did not win for him the fashion honours of the evening. They went to Faye Dunaway, star of *Bonnie and Clyde*, who arrived in a thirties-style brown satin maxi-coat, trimmed with ostrich feathers.

As on all his memorable occasions, Harris never forgot his own people. There were relatives and friends from Limerick; Harmay, his sister who was still very close to him, came; and his wife Elizabeth wasn't forgotten – she was accompanied by actor Christopher Plummer, with whom she was having a relationship at the time. At the dinner after the première, Plummer sat on the left of Princess Margaret and Harris sat on her right. He had been instructed not to speak until he was spoken to, which seemed a tall order for a compulsive talker.

During the second course, to general consternation, he could no longer remain silent. Turning to the Princess he said, 'Ma'am, am I invisible?' He went on to assure her that she would find him much more interesting than the man on her left with whom she had been talking exclusively.

The Princess laughed politely as he went on to talk good-humouredly about Irishmen, English women and Protestants. He was still on a high after the rapturous reception accorded *Camelot* at its première earlier, and eager for conversation.

The evening was a most civilized affair. After the dinner, Harris invited his wife Elizabeth and Christopher Plummer to join his relatives and friends back at his Chesham Place flat. Elizabeth recalls, 'The evening ended amicably enough with all of us gathered around the piano while Chris played songs from *Camelot*.'

In subsequent days, his telephone never ceased ringing as Fleet Street columnists sought interviews. He was on the crest of the wave, but to the more discerning journalists he remained a puzzle. They could not, even at this stage of his tumultuous career, reconcile the ambitious star with the hard-drinking, irresponsible hellraiser. Why did he do it? What, at the age of thirty-four, was he still trying to prove?

'I feel good inside when I drink,' was his answer. 'Drink makes me feel warm. It makes me feel mellow.'

It was partly true, as it was true in the case of Burton, O'Toole, Reed and Trevor Howard. There were also other reasons, of course. Perhaps, as a life-long rebel he was angry with the world, or, even more so, his drinking betrayed his personal unhappiness. In the next breath he said, 'I drink when I'm happy, when I'm with friends. It's boredom, frustration, not drink, that makes me aggressive.'

He was proud of his success in *Camelot* which the *New York Times* described as 'the £5 million tapestry of misty castle, galloping knights in armour, duels, jousting matches and magic tricks', though Gerard O'Reilly, film critic of the *Evening Herald*, was to comment, 'The stumbling-block in this magnificent spectacle is the ponderous script, which takes its graver moments too turgidly and in its gayer moments strives too hard for laughter.'

Critic Pauline Kael wrote of the movie in the *New Yorker*.

One of Hollywood's colossal financial disasters. The film of the Lerner-and-Lowe musical got so expensively big that it went out of control; the sets and people and costumes seem to be sitting there on the screen, waiting for the unifying magic that never happens. The picture wavers in tone, but it does have good bits tucked in among the elaborate mistakes. It has a fascination; it's like a huge ruin that makes one wonder what the blueprints could possibly have indicated. It's hard to guess what the director, Joshua Logan, was aiming at. Richard Harris's King Arthur is eccentric and unfathomable in the first half, but he achieves some powerful moments later on; Vanessa Redgrave, flying high, is a puzzling but spectacular Guinevere ...'

To Harris, it would always remain more than a movie or a musical. It had helped steer his career in another vital direction and thus gave him a new dimension. Every time he heard *Camelot* songs on radio, or heard them sung on television, he knew that he wanted to become a recording artist – a pop star.

Already, his career was moving in that direction. But there were still more films to do. Rich and famous, he could now afford to be more selective.

13   *A spy in Pennsylvania*

He had been accused occasionally of being rude to his leading ladies but, if he was, Harris could also be intensely loyal to them. In conversation, he spoke warmly of Rachel Roberts, Doris Day, Vanessa Redgrave – and even Princess Soraya. His latest, Samantha Eggar, would star with him in *The Molly Maguires*. Martin Ritt's £3.5 million production set among the Irish immigrant coal-miners in Pennsylvania in the 1870s.

In the movie, Harris is cast as McPherson, a management spy hired to infiltrate the Molly Maguires, a secret organization who have been dynamiting the trains carrying the coal they have just mined. He eventually befriends miners' leader (Sean Connery) and is won over by the sincerity of the oppressed. The story was written by Ritt's life-long friend Walter Bernstein and, although based on fact, the plot is pure fiction.

Connery had finished filming *Shalako* that April 1968, and almost without a break he flew to Pennsylvania to begin making *The Molly Maguires*. He was anxious to confirm that he was free from the Bond straitjacket. This had not been achieved without some friction and included a libel action by a French newspaper that he eventually won. A man of independent views, he counted the flamboyant Harris among his friends. He didn't mind taking second billing in *The Molly Maguires*, for, as he said, 'They're paying me a million dollars for this picture. For that money they can put a mule ahead of me.'

When Harris got the Bernstein script he liked the two-level dimension of his own character McPherson who was both tough and weak. The role, as in the case of Connery, also afforded him an opportunity to get away from King Arthur and his regal image. Shooting the movie in Pennsylvania he reckoned would invest it with authentic atmosphere and make it a valuable period piece.

During the duration of the movie Samantha Eggar rented a house for herself and her two small children. Her husband Tom Stern was away house-hunting in California in preparation for their move back to Hollywood. Five years before, Samantha had scored a big success in *The Collector* but since then the memory of her freckles and red hair had faded at the box office. She had tried to push herself back to centre stage with *Walk, Don't Run*, but despite Cary Grant's starring role the film flopped.

Harris and Connery called her Sam. Together, they took off for a reconstructed ghost town in Pennsylvania. 'Sam was terribly suspicious of Sean and myself at the beginning,' recalls Harris, 'and tremendously on the defensive because she'd had a rough time on earlier films. Women are more exposed to roughness, you know. She's sensitive and she hurts easily. Her background had made her very proud, very proper, not able to communicate openly at first. So she adopted this stand-off quality as a defence mechanism – and also the bitchiness people talked about, though I'd never experienced it in her.'

At first, Samantha wasn't too popular with the cast and crew who found her somewhat aloof. Harris was to notice it but said nothing. 'After about ten days,' he says, 'I had trouble with a scene. So I asked Sean what I was doing wrong, and he helped me through. I think Sam was amazed to see two actors of our calibre helping each other, not trying to upstage each other. And she relaxed. Once we got to know her she became the absolute darling of the crew. They adored her.'

To Harris and the others, she looked fragile, as though she was going to fall to pieces, but he suspected that she was as gutsy as they said she was. He remembered her from a few years back, when she visited him once ... 'glowing red hair and a delicate beauty that photographed marvellously'.

To Samantha, Harris had the power to generate excitement and loosen the complexes of people around him. He had a powerful presence both as man and actor and in her view was far from the simple caricature of the drinking Irishman. 'He pours out so much energy that you simply have to try to match up to him,' she said. 'Mad as Richard is, when he says something, he means it.'

'It was a happy movie to make,' recalls Connery. 'Working with Richard was an experience.' It was also a tough schedule for both actors, but they were physically fit and full of energy.

One scene in the movie called for a reproduction of what was supposed to be a friendly game, an 1876 football match which was a sort of roughshod cross between soccer and rugby. Harris led one team and Connery the other, having refused to allow doubles to take their places.

Soon they wished they had allowed the doubles. Players were left strewn across the pitch as though it had been a battlefield. Well, it had been a battle. Harris came off the pitch with a black eye, a broken nose and sore ribs, and as for Connery himself, he had twisted his right knee and badly bruised his shoulder. Even the Irish referee, Malachy McCourt, who by now ran a bar in New York called 'Himself', had been kicked in the beard in the process of the game, thereby impairing his judgement.

'It was bloody hell out there on that pitch,' recalled the boisterous McCourt. 'Richard Harris must have thought he was back again in *Sporting Life*.'

The bearded McCourt loved Harris's ribald humour and no-nonsense approach to life. 'The guy's got more talent in his little finger than a score of other actors I know,' he'd say. Together, they drank, swore, retailed funny stories and indulged in mad escapades. 'The Ginger Man wasn't in it with us,' says McCourt.

When eventually it was released, *The Molly Maguires* received mixed notices from the critics. In the case of Connery, Kevin Collins, the *Irish Times* critic, wrote:

In the end, the problem with this film was the actor's apparent inaction, the fact that he seemed merely to be occupying screen space, dourly staring into the middle distance, that rumbling baritone the only potent reminder of an earlier warmth and intensity.

Pauline Kael devoted a good deal of space in the *New Yorker* to a review of the movie. She commented:

The Molly Maguires is a failure, nailed on its own aspirations to the tragic and the epic, yet it's an impressive failure. It's not a movie one can work up much enthusiasm for, but it's not a negligible movie. In the end, it is too sombre and portentous for the rather dubious story it carries, but it feels like a reminder of a bitter, tragic past and when you come away you know you've seen something.

Ms Kael agreed, though, that it was beautifully made and full of atmosphere.

But the movie not only has a look, it's acted with great intensity, and it focusses on a figure who is generally given only marginal treatment in this kind of material – the company spy ... Richard Harris, whose devious, hangdog expression makes him a natural for the role, is wily and complex as a smart but weak man. He has a volatile edginess that draws us into the spy's divided spirit and contributes most of the suspense in the film. And Samantha Eggar is surprisingly forceful as the girl who becomes the fiancée of the stool pigeon.

'I think Sam was marvellous in the movie,' recalled Harris. 'She brought an indefinable quality to her role, just what Martin Ritt wanted.' At first, he was inclined to be carried away by the merits of the movie and was quoted as saying, 'I think it's one of the great movies of my life, really, and I don't always like my own films.'

However, on reflection, he was to say, 'To me *The Molly Maguires* was a heartbreaking experience. It was not the movie that I agreed to make. I set out to make a movie about a subject which was very much a part of Martin Ritt's background, and I knew he was dedicated to it. It was a story of an Irish informer who joined the Molly Maguires in the Pennsylvania coalmining district in 1870. Ritt took the story and related it to those people who had betrayed his own kind during the McCarthy witchhunt. Ritt was very bitter about this period and wanted to make the film as a personal statement. He was also attempting something even more subtle: he was exposing the treachery on which America exists and the men who climb any kind of ladder to reach the top. His Mister Success would be an Irishman who gets off the boat willing to do anything to become successful, even betray the people he loves. He believes the issues at stake are right, but because he is alone he has no choice except to become an informer. When I saw Ritt's first version of the movie it was shattering and brutal, intellectually brutal; but, because of whatever pressures one must assume were placed on Ritt during the editing, the film was watered down. The film became a great compromise on the screen in which one was never involved.'

As the 1970s approached, Harris was giving more thought to movie-making and the industry itself. He had by now formed certain views, not all of them popular with the tycoons who ran the business. In the movie industry he said that one was subject to a gigantic machine which had no interest in good performances. The men who operated the machine were interested in getting one's name into a movie in the hope that people would want to see you, but never for the reasons that you might be good or bad in it or for what you might be trying to achieve. Giant corporations had taken over the studios in America and were out to make money for motion pictures. Their bosses sat in on 'rushes' and criticized matters they knew nothing about. A director could demand the right to the first cut, so they gave it to him because it was obligatory. But once he had presented his movie they had the right to change it.

'A producer or director may use me to fight the studios,' he added, 'but no matter how much fuss I make they'll put out the version they think fit. Despite the shouting, they will claim it is their nine million dollars; and, indeed, with such financial investment involved they have the right to make changes.'

It was becoming clear that he was seriously thinking about directing his own movie. In technical terms, he had come a long way since he played a small part in the James Cagney movie, *Shake Hands with the Devil*. Furthermore, he had an opportunity to see some of the great directors at work, including John Huston. They had awakened a new interest in him and he would not be happy until he achieved that new ambition.

With his endless stamina and eagerness to try out new ideas, he began to pursue a career in singing, and took the jumpy world of pop music by storm when 'MacArthur Park' was released: inside four weeks it had climbed to No. 3 in the charts and sold 600,000 copies; soon afterwards *A Tramp Shining* was in the Top Twenty.

The inspiration behind the songs was young American

composer Jim Webb. 'Richard could have made it as a great singer if he wasn't being an actor,' says Webb. 'I really mean that.'

When someone said that Harris had a voice that sounded like coal being shovelled, he shrugged his massive shoulders and carried on writing his own song compositions. His venture into pop had saved him some fancy psychiatric fees, it was said at the time, but singing also gave him a new and lucrative interest and underlined his versatility as an artist. 'I'm prepared to try anything new,' he would say. 'In that way I never let myself get bored.'

Elizabeth Harris believed in him as a singer and did not mind when he wrote one number called 'Didn't We Girl?' which dealt with their estrangement. 'The song tells of our parting and our three or four attempts to come together again,' Harris himself explained. 'I've played the music to Elizabeth and she said it was okay by her.'

At her home in Kensington, she played his records for her three children and friends. 'Richard's got a marvellous voice,' she mused. She was intensely proud of his latest achievement, although not as surprised as people thought. She had suspected for a long time that he was multi-talented and in this respect had not been given the credit he deserved. One felt that she had always admired rather than condemned the antics of her headstrong husband. 'Life was never dull,' she would say, remembering the black eyes, the abuse, the fits of temperament that became as much her husband's trademark as his films'.

She had found independence and peace. But she had no regrets. 'Richard is a wonderful person,' she said with feeling. 'I can admire him now from a distance.' Their life together had been as unpredictable as his moods. 'Sometimes he would go out of the house for a short walk,' she remembered, 'and decide he'd like to see his family in Ireland, and come home two weeks later. He always carries his toothbrush with him – and I knew that as long as he had his toothbrush he was packed to go anywhere.'

Visitors to her home found that as the months went on she talked more nostalgically about her ex-husband. They found it hard to tell whether she was pleased or sorry that they were finally parted for good. Suddenly, she would say, 'Listen, I'll play something from *A Tramp Shining*.' Silence would follow as everyone listened intently as Richard's voice filled the sitting-room. Her face would light up and a look of nostalgia would come into her eyes. At that moment she knew in a strange way, that he hadn't left their home in Kensington, when of course he had.

That July 1969, they had officially divorced, and Elizabeth decided to rebuild her life. In a few months she would begin seeing a lot of Rex Harrison who, by now, was separated from his wife Rachel Roberts. When confronted by Rachel and asked, 'Are you in love with Rex?', Elizabeth replied, 'Yes, I am.'

Harris himself reacted unpredictably to the divorce. The occasion, he decided, called for a long weekend's celebration. A Honeymoon without a Bride, he called it. In place of a bride were six guests intent on merriment, and waiting at London Airport, an eight-seater Falcon jet on hire to Harris to take him anywhere he fancied.

It was typical of his hellraising spirit, and his 'groomsman' Malachy McCourt was there to ensure that the fun never waned. For three days they intended to tour the night clubs, strip clubs and bars of the Continent. One reporter, who was brave enough to cover the tour, reported, 'Days were to scream crazily into nights and nights were to belch horribly back into days.'

The 'honeymoon' began with champagne in Harris's Rolls-Royce on the way to the airport and a mad trolley race through the airport corridors past astonished passengers. Once aboard the jet Harris took stock of his recruits. Beside him sat the bearded Malachy McCourt who reckoned that a celebration was the best possible way for Richard to get over his divorce trauma. 'I don't want him to cry crocodile tears,' said McCourt, 'I want him to laugh at the world. It's not the end of the world for Richard. He's big enough to take the blows.'

To McCourt, it was important to be with his boozing pal during the actor's most traumatic time in a decade. 'I'm sure the celebration helped Richard to forget the most painful parts of the divorce,' he said later. 'By the time it was all over he was too exhausted to get worked up about it. It was the bloody tonic he needed.'

Friends began to worry whether Harris would come to rely on alcohol to forget the emptiness around him, although he would be able to see his three sons. To the world he hadn't changed; he was still wild, unpredictable and talented. As a personality, he stood head and shoulders above most of his colleagues and his energetic approach to life was awesome. His periodic binges were his way of purging the alcohol inside him, and then it was back to work, composing songs, reading scripts, jotting down lines of poetry ... and, of course, telling stories.

14   'Who is Mister Cromwell?'

'Who is Mister Cromwell?' they asked in America.

'Mister ... Cromwell ...?'

'Gee, Mister Hughes ... we'd like to know.'

Hughes shook his head despairingly. 'He's ... not ... Mister Cromwell ... exactly ... He's ... Oliver Cromwell.'

Director/scriptwriter Ken Hughes was on a promotional tour for Columbia Pictures to stimulate interest in *Cromwell*, which starred Richard Harris in the title role, with Alec Guinness as King Charles I. He was astonished to find so little interest in the historical seventeenth-century figure; worse, he met some Americans who had never heard of Cromwell. It was one of the main reasons to which he attributed the box-office failure of the movie in the States.

Cromwell, which had been shot on location in England, Spain and Ireland in the late 1960s, ran for three months at the Odeon, Leicester Square, broke box-office records in Continental cinemas, and did brisk business in Australia. 'Americans just didn't care a damn about Oliver Cromwell,' says Hughes, 'and many of them didn't want to know. I had sympathy for Richard Harris and Alec Guinness who had put such a lot into their parts. In my view, it is one of the best things Harris has ever done on screen.'

Hughes today lives in Hollywood, but retains vivid memories of making the movie. In the 1960s, he lived in London and became better known after he had directed Laurence Harvey and Kim Novak in *Of Human Bondage*. 'My relationship with Kim Novak went from instant love to instant hate,' he recalls. 'She was pretty tempestuous.' He found Harvey temperamental, but less of a headache.

Harris, he says was his first choice to play the title role in *Cromwell*. The actor was in Hollywood at that time and came across the film script in a producer's office and immediately sent a cable to Hughes in London: 'I WANT TO PLAY THE PART OF CROM-WELL. I'D LOVE TO DO THIS FILM.'

It was the old Harris determination asserting itself, reminiscent of his approach to Joshua Logan, the director of *Camelot*. Clearly he would not take no for an answer.

Hughes had never met Harris but, on his own admission, was terrified of his reputation. 'I think he frightened me at the time,' he recalls. 'I mean, some of his off-screen antics seemed to overshadow his professional career. But this image didn't deter me from giving him the role of Cromwell.'

To Hughes, the actor saw more than politics in the part. The powerful conflict on a more human level between Cromwell and the King intrigued him. He was ideal for the part. Harris laughed when the director suggested jokily that 'No self-respecting Irishman should play Cromwell.'

Hughes's script caught the mood of the period. The film opens in 1640 when Parliament has not assembled for twelve years. Cromwell is about to take off for America due to his disillusionment with the political scene, but decides instead to fight for his beliefs. Parliament is reassembled, but refuses to grant the King the money he needs for his wars and signs the death warrant of the tyrannical Earl of Strafford (Patrick Wymark). The fight is on. In gripping battle scenes Charles's troops are triumphant at Edgehill and then, after a period of intense training, the film follows the victory of Cromwell at Naseby in 1645. The King is on the gloomy path to the executioner's block.

Hughes was no longer frightened of the Harris hellraising image. On the contrary, he found the actor totally professional on the film set. He had faced more problems in *Of Human Bondage*. One thing surprised him, and it was how nervous Harris appeared in his first scene with Alec Guinness. 'I think Richard was a little overawed by Alec's reputation as an actor. I mean, he was a legend in the business.'

The director's only real problem arose at the editing stage when the Company decided to cut out altogether the bloody scenes of Cromwell's sacking of Drogheda during his Irish campaign. He and his army arrived in Ireland in 1649 to quell the civil war raging in the country, but the way he went about it underlined the utterly ruthless side of his character. Historically, the campaign has become a *cause célèbre* in Irish history.

Hughes challenged Columbia on their decision to dispense with the scenes on the grounds that they were not only important to the film itself but an integral part of history. 'They wouldn't listen to me,' he recalls. 'I fought them tooth and nail over the question. I felt audiences were being cheated by omitting the scenes.'

Likewise, Harris was both surprised and disappointed by the company's arbitrary decision. 'From my point of view,' he says, 'they were among the best scenes we shot. I was happy with my own portrayal of Cromwell and count the movie among the best I have done.'

He had other reasons to remember it. On his own admission he had been drinking rather heavily around that time, although he never once arrived drunk on the set. He received warning signs when he began one day to hallucinate; he became frightened and decided to cut down on the alcohol – and see a psychiatrist. When he told friends his experience, they begged him to ease up or cut out drinking altogether. It was a difficult time in his life; there was no Elizabeth around with whom to spar verbally, and at night he sometimes stayed late at nightclubs or eating places.

'I wasn't much interested in the private side of Richard's life,' says Hughes. 'Directors don't have the time to worry about that side unless it leads to problems on the film set. We became friendly and I never thought of his hellraising image again.'

Sir Alec Guinness was polite and helpful to Harris, but tended to keep to himself. He is not a gregarious man. Ken Hughes felt that no other actor could have carried off the role of King Charles as did Guinness. 'He was wonderful.'

Cromwell received enthusiastic notices. Critic Ian Christie commented,

> Here, for once we have an historical epic that excites the imagination and stirs the emotions without insulting the intelligence. A first-class film by any standards that brings a period of history vividly to life and dramatises the political antagonisms of the mid-seventeenth century in a way that had me enthralled for its entire two hours and nineteen minutes.

Christie thought Harris made Cromwell into a formidable heroic figure, inspired by his religious faith and belief in justice for the common man to oppose the might of King Charles I and the corruption of the Parliament that followed his execution.

Whether wielding his sword in battle or dominating politicians by the strength of his personality and the courage of his convictions [he continued], Harris gives a magnificent, commanding performance. But the film is by no means a one-man show. With Alec Guinness as King Charles, the intransigence of the monarchy that was responsible for civil war and finally the triumph of the democratic system is brought home forcibly.

Critics praised Ken Hughes's script, and one pointed out, 'The dialogue actually sounds as if it could have been uttered by living human beings, and his direction is firm but unobtrusive.'

The American view, by contrast, was less laudatory. Critic Pauline Kael posed the question:

Was there ever a period of history when the clothes were less photogenic? The actors waddle around in their barrels and bloomers, then stand still to make speeches at each other.

She described Harris 'of the hangdog expression' as

a star not by virtue of public appeal but simply because he's such a domineering powerhouse that he seems a natural for important roles ... [He played Cromwell, she said] with glum, frowning righteousness, using his weird straight eyebrows like punctuation marks. And not only are his lines flat, but there is no music in his voice. Is this a movie about a great national *hero*? If virtue is as toneless as this Cromwell, who wouldn't prefer vice?

Miss Kael summed up, 'Shakespeare spoiled us for this sort of thing; we waited for great speeches and witty remarks, for rage and poetry, and we get nothing but a relentless academicism.'

Director Ken Hughes wasn't impressed by some of the

criticism of Harris and thought it was unreasonable. 'The fact is most of the critics liked Richard in the role,' he recalls.

With such a hectic film schedule, Harris had scarcely time to read what the critics said about his performances, never mind worry about them. That December in 1969 he was on location in Mexico filming *A Man Called Horse* for Cinema Centre Films.

It is 1825 and Harris plays a young English aristocrat who goes to America and is captured by Sioux Indians while on a hunting expedition. The Indians make him into a slave. Before, he had wealth and social position. Now he is naked and degraded.

For the star, the movie was a challenge. 'It is a breakthrough in the cinema's treatment of nudity,' he said. 'This is the unclothed body used to make a valid dramatic point, in keeping with the story's primitive setting.'

Even more surprising, though, is that the nude scenes here have nothing to do with sex. It was considered one of the boldest departures in film-making at that time. Said one American critic, '*A Man Called Horse* gives Richard Harris a dramatic role within which he is able to totally reveal his physical assets in a way never before open to an actor.' Later, it did extremely well at the box-office in America. 'I count it among my best half-dozen movies,' says Harris. 'It was simply different.'

He harboured some regrets about projects that did not come off for some reason or other. Dylan Thomas, as man and poet, appealed to him tremendously and for a long time he hoped to do a show around his turbulent and sad life. He was able to recite some of his poetry and had read a great deal about him, but he was unable to get the project off the ground.

'I regard Dylan Thomas as a great poet,' he would say. 'His story should be screened or presented as a solo show on stage.' Being himself acquainted with alcohol, he identified with the dilemma that faced the poet, especially in America. By the late Sixties he hadn't despaired of doing the project.

He was also interested in screening the life of colourful Irish patriot, Michael Collins, about whose life and political career at least six books have been written. It was a question of time and money and just now his film schedule was too busy to devote time to Collins.

He was seldom out of the news. Even when he hugged a blonde traffic warden innocently in the street it made headlines. On this occasion the woman did not consider it funny. Harris had had a few lunchtime drinks in Belgravia and when he saw her writing down the number of a car owned by a friend of his he folded his arms around the woman to prevent her writing down the number. She got free but he held her several times. Then he danced around between her and the car. He was summoned for assault.

Harris, who pleaded not guilty, told the court, 'The traffic warden seemed as if she was taking the whole thing as a joke. I never touched her. The only thing I did was to dance an Irish jig in front of her. I thought she was a good audience.'

The magistrate wasn't amused. 'You must not go around thinking that everyone enjoys being hugged,' he told the star. 'It was misplaced friendliness on your part.'

Harris was given a six-month conditional discharge. The case underlined that despite approaching forty he was still full of fun and mischief-making. As ever, life, in his book, was there to be lived – or lived up. He hated the cautious and conventional approach.

Sometimes it was his quick temper, aggravated by alcohol that got him into trouble. Once, during a performance by his friend, Sammy Davis Junior, in London's Talk of the Town restaurant, he took exception to remarks made by a man about Jews. The singer ignored the remark, but Harris and the other man went outside and came to blows.

Two police officers tried to calm the two men and were assaulted. Harris was taken away to the police station. The next morning he pleaded guilty to obstructing a police officer and was fined. He said that for the previous six months he had been working on a film and this was his first night off, and he had been drinking.

After the case, he said he asked the man in the restaurant twice to be quiet. 'In the end I hit him. I know Sammy Davis very well.'

He was used by now to living with controversy and, understandably, took it all in his stride. In 1969, when he walked out of the movie *Play It Dirty* on location in Spain, he had a sound reason it seemed. As he explained, 'There was no mystery. I left Spain on Saturday and returned to London today.

The script I was handed in America was not the script I had seen in London.'

The film was being produced by Harry Saltzman, producer of the Bond films, and concerned a group of soldiers operating behind German lines in North Africa in 1943. It would have featured Harris and Michael Caine.

Quizzed further about his early departure from Spain, he said, 'There is no truth in the story that I refused to take off my moustache and sideburns. It was stipulated before I accepted the film that I should take them off. I had promised director Martin Ritt that I would not appear in this with them.'

Harris threatened to sue the film company for the equivalent of his fee. He was normally paid about £200,000 for a film. A spokesman for Lowndes Productions said he knew of Mr Harris's comments – 'but we would not be prepared to say anything'.

Aidan Hennigan, London editor of an Irish morning newspaper, was friendly with Harris at that time and was among the journalists who sometimes telephoned the star to seek confirmation of show-biz stories. Once, he was invited to dinner at the star's garden flat in Chesham Place, Belgravia. He remembers the scene that greeted him.

We sat around a 16th-century oak table in a darkish room. Flickering candles played strange tricks on the walls. Richard talked about acting, religion, politics and personal convictions. He is a restless man, intense, often preoccupied. Ideas bubble forth in a curious sort of monologue. He paces up and down, invites you to listen to his records, asks you to have a drink, sips soda water as if he is not drinking and worries a little about his health.

What intrigued him was Harris's attire.

He wore a black collarless tunic shirt buttoned up to the neck. He had a brown table napkin tucked under his chin. His acquiline nose set in a rather ascetic face was accentuated by the candlelight. It was as if I was sitting opposite a United States cavalry officer.

To Hennigan, it was akin to a theatrical setting and one he had not quite expected. He felt that Harris's reputation as a fire-brand and hellraiser was exaggerated, though he could not say for certain. Listening to the star talking in an incredibly soft voice it was hard for him to imagine him a hellraiser.

As the evening wore on, and he listened to his philosophy of life, and his music, Hennigan was a little puzzled by Harris's combination of personal charm, intensity, fine mind, and a certain irascibility.

'I felt that success had not spoiled him,' he says today, and decided the actor was more intelligent than he was given credit for. He had not lost sight of himself, and was not likely to, despite fame, booze and controversy.

15 *Football star in decline*

Superstar, pop star, poet and songwriter, raconteur, quintessential Irishman – in that year, 1970, it looked an imposing list of credits and clearly illustrated that despite his reputation Harris was achieving most of his ambitions. He had never lost sight of his professional career, even if on occasions he got above himself with unhappy consequences.

Soon he would add, if rather fortuitously, to the increasing list. It came about when he went to Israel to star in *Bloomfield*, a movie about a soccer star in decline. After ten days' shooting, the director resigned and Harris was urged to take over direction. He could not, he felt, say no.

The storyline appealed to his sports sense. 'The man,' he reflected, 'has put everything he has into his playing career and has given no thought to what will happen when he reaches forty and is finished. He doesn't care. He has existed only for sport. Everyone else sees what is going to happen to him. And everyone deserts him. It is pathetic. It's autobiographical.'

In his eyes, the movie was a new challenge, something he had never done before. The only direction he had ever attempted was at the London Academy of Music and Dramatic Art, when he directed scenes from Shaw's *St Joan* and Miller's *Death of a Salesman*. Although he had enjoyed the experience, it was of no possible help to him in film directing. He began to sit up at night planning and rewriting the scenes for the following day. When they had rescheduled the shooting he realized he could not be back in London in time to play in the movie *Scrooge*. His producer did not want him to lose $600,000 and was willing for him to shoot the end of *Bloomfield* after he had made *Scrooge*, but this would have meant handing over the editing of his movie to somebody else and Harris was not prepared to do that. He decided, therefore, to turn down the role.

As he said, 'I know famous directors who hand over their work when they have finished directing. They see the editor once a week and make suggestions while they're doing other jobs, and then they believe they have cut the movies. But you must be there every day and look at every frame. You must supervise the laying of the soundtrack and the dubbing of the music, otherwise you have no right to call it your movie. In a way you place your head on the block because you must assume you are always right.'

It was reassuring at least for him to begin direction of *Bloomfield* with the experience gained from working with good directors, which stood him in good stead. 'I think the crew imagined I wasn't going to do it, or if I did it would be an actor's brief indulgence in direction. We shot for sixteen weeks on a budget of $1½ million dollars. I had never worked on such an inexpensive movie in my career. My previous three movies had cost $28 million between them. But once I began to go through the accounts on *Bloomfield* I realized the fantastic wastage in the industry. When you see the end product on the screen you wonder how it could have cost so many million dollars.'

He admitted he broke the rules making *Bloomfield*. 'Whenever they told me something was impossible I wanted to know why. I had no preparation before the film began, because I did not know I would be directing.'

A lame script allied to unimaginative direction was mainly the reason put forward for the artistic failure of *Bloomfield*. One could add to this Harris's own lack of conviction in the central role of Eitan, the failed footballer, though it was felt that having to direct as well as act was in his case asking too much. It has to be said that the only thing impressive about the movie was the superb camerawork.

Although he said later that he would like to do more directing, he was unhappy with the end result in *Bloomfield* and was determined never again to direct as well as act in a movie. 'I just didn't have the time to prepare things properly,' he explained. 'I like the idea, though, of directing because I love the poetic expression you get with movies.'

He was never afraid to be self-critical of his own film and stage performances. He believed it was absolutely necessary to ensure high artistic standards. Working with the best professionals in the business fired his imagination and renewed his energy; he despised shoddy work. Although, on his own admission, *Bloomfield* was disappointing as a movie, he cared passionately about it and made no secret of the fact that he had put £300,000 of his own money into it.

When he flew to Berlin for the showing of the film, he was dismayed by the hostile reception and ended up being booed and booing the audience right back. He could still be pugnacious with a purpose.

Earlier in the month, he had arranged that his home town Limerick should stage the world première of *Bloomfield*. It was a thoughtful gesture by the star and in keeping with his accepted spirit of generosity. The screening would be in aid of handicapped children.

Like most things he did, Harris ensured the occasion would not be without its razzamatazz and excitement. It was after all a unique occasion. Limerick's own movie star was returning as star of his own movie. Typically, he decided to arrive in style. He hired a chartered plane and with a party of London friends arrived at the Savoy Cinema via Shannon Airport. His party included singing star Lulu, actress Honor Blackman, and Kim Burfield, the boy star of the movie.

There was a touch of irony about Harris's grand entry to the cinema. Heads turned as he was whisked inside the building where he was once barred because of his pranks. Now, wearing a maxi-length suede coat, he acknowledged the cheers of the crowd. 'Good God! it's Dickie Harris!' one old man was heard to exclaim above the heads of the crowd, as though reluctant to accept that the wild young boy he once knew was returning a hero.

It was true, and everyone else in Limerick acknowledged that the city could claim its first movie star. Inside the cinema more than 1,500 people waited for the screening, happy in the knowledge that Harris and his party had arrived safely. However, at 8.30 an anonymous caller telephoned the Garda headquarters and a male voice said that a bomb had been planted under one of the seats of the cinema. As the building was being searched by gardai and detectives, the audience, including Harris and his friends, filed out hurriedly into the street. It was another thirty minutes before they were re-admitted.

'There was a lot of confusion,' recalls Bill Whelan, 'and a lot of excitement. I could not find my parents in the pushing to get out.' At nineteen, he was one of the youngest music composers in Ireland, and *Bloomfield* had helped him gain some international recognition.

Months earlier, he had sent a piece of music to Harris's music company in London and shortly afterwards got a telephone call from Dermot Harris that his brother Richard was interested.

'Richard rang me later,' Whelan remembers, 'and said he liked the score and that it caught the mood of the theme of a film they wanted to do. I met him in Limerick and we went to a hotel in Kilkee to do further work on the music score for *Bloomfield*. I was told it would be completed and orchestrated in London by Johnny Harris.'

Whelan believed that Richard Harris owed a lot to Jim Webb who was at that time influential in his career as a pop star. 'I loved "Macarthur Park" and the two LPs Webb did with Richard,' he said. He had no great voice but in my view he was a good dramatic interpreter of a song. I wasn't surprised at all by his pop success.'

After the audience was shown to their seats there were no further hitches to the première of *Bloomfield*. Limerick, being a great sport-loving city, identified with the hero of the movie and at the final curtain Harris and his friends were accorded warm applause.

'There was an undoubted buzz in the cinema,' recalls Bill Whelan. 'Afterwards Richard Harris gave us a very good time.' No one seemed to worry about the limitations of the movie, the excitement of the occasion was all that mattered.

Commented Harris, 'As I entered the Savoy Cinema I thought I should still be barred from coming in here. Some of the staff there were still the same as barred me years before, so it was a bit touch and go as to whether I'd be allowed inside!'

Before they left Limerick, Honor Blackman and the rest of the party had become familiar with Dickie Harris and the legends that had grown up about him. Somehow they didn't dismiss them. They knew that anything was possible where he was concerned. For his own part, the occasion revived memories. There was the time years before when he saw *Wuthering Heights*, starring Merle Oberon, at the local Carlton Cinema and instantly fell in love with the star.

'Words could not describe how I felt about her,' he says. 'She was really beautiful. I went to every film the woman ever appeared in and developed a teenage fascination for her. I was her greatest fan and became so completely infatuated with her that it worried me.'

At night, he remembered, he lay awake thinking about her. He had photographs of her and not a moment passed when he did not have a new erotic fantasy about her. It was months before he got over the deep infatuation.

Yet despite his sexual fantasies, he never forgot his southern Irish roots; they were vitally important to him. He had by now bought a house in Kilkee, the seaside resort he loved like a child, for it evoked memories of his wild youth as he danced, drank, sang and kissed the pretty girls. He rarely visited his house there, but in a strange way its presence gave him a sense of belonging. A sense of happiness and an awareness of the past, something he assured himself he could never find elsewhere.

It was a troubled time in Ireland. He talked of solutions to the Northern Ireland problem and pleaded, 'For God's sake let's learn to live in peace.' But he was in danger of being misunderstood by the Fleet Street press: when he talked of Irish nationalism, a few of them accused him of being in sympathy with IRA violence. Nothing was further from the truth. Soon it seemed a mistake for him to get involved in a part of Ireland that the *Sunday Times* was describing as 'a political slum'. Yet it inspired him to write a poem of peace which was published widely.

He had no reason, he said, to be disillusioned about Ireland. He liked being Irish and he could say he had found no prejudice against the Irish in London. By nature he was nomadic. He liked to travel and move in different areas among different peoples. 'I like to keep moving, and this in a way is the Irish thing. I'm proud to be called an Irishman. Why not? I'm not ashamed.'

On his return from America he had read in the *Evening Standard* that Liberace had bought Tower House in London. He telephoned the agents immediately and described the house in detail and his part in successfully prevailing on the National Trust to preserve it. They met him at the house early in the morning and in a short time he had signed a cheque for £75,000 and the house was his. Liberace had not put down the deposit, so he beat him to it.

'When I go into Tower House and close the door behind me I might be anywhere,' he mused.

It held nostalgic memories for him. As he recalled, 'When I had no place to sleep in London in the 1950s I found this doomed Gothic Victorian house in Medbury Road one night. It was strange, but absolutely beautiful and I loved it straight away. For many nights I slept beneath a tree in the garden. When I visited it later it was a shambles inside. Statues and walls had been desecrated.'

Harris had made a study of Tower House and formed the impression that William Burgess, who built it, was a man of genius in design, but his weakness was that he did not know how to display his house. He cluttered the place up and one couldn't see the walls for furniture.

To his friends – and the gossip columnists – the big house seemed somewhat empty without a woman. The ebullient Harris, who was aware that he had acquired a new status symbol to go with his Rolls-Royce, was not reluctant to talk about himself, now that Elizabeth was about to marry Rex Harrison.

'I've been analysing my activities over the past two years,' he said, 'and I've come to the conclusion that what I like about love is the tragedy of it all. If the relationship shows the slightest signs of not becoming tragic, I make it. As soon as I meet a girl, even before we have our first date, I've already worked out how it will end. I can't tell you how disheartened I'd be if a love affair didn't end tragically.'

For the first time he reflected openly on his marriage to Elizabeth. 'If I'm to be honest,' he said, 'I gave nothing in my marriage to Elizabeth. Only what was easy: a house, a car, a coat – the things men give because they're not prepared to give any more.'

Perhaps his unusual attitude to women could be found in his own words: 'I need a woman to haunt me. A woman to tear my insides out. It's never happened, and that's sad. Or rather, I've never allowed it to happen. Every time there's been the slightest hint that it might, I'm off, leaving her to haunt someone else.'

He had been asked on the *David Frost Show* in America

whether he ever felt the pangs of loneliness, and he had replied that if he hadn't been lonely a lot he wouldn't have written any poetry.

Of his future he said, 'I have to contemplate the day when no one is going to ask me to act in a movie. I don't give a damn. I might last, like Tracy or Cooper. I don't think about tomorrow because I'm not interested in ten years' time. If you do, you become that age. You can worry yourself into an older frame of mind.'

He argued that if there was a place for regrets in one's life then there was something wrong. 'You are living today and you must be part of that, even if part of that includes failure.'

Significantly, he continued to talk of his ambition to do a film version of *Hamlet*, as though it were the only Shakespearean character that interested him. He saw aspects of himself in the man, in his varying moods and introspection, and the eloquence of the language captivated him. As yet this ambition had not become an obsession with him. He decided it could wait for a little while longer.

Someone wrote in the middle of 1970 that his wild image seemed to be dying away. It was of course too early to predict. It was perhaps closer to the mark to say, 'He is respectably opinionated' or 'One senses a solitary man beneath the bravura.' Undoubtedly he had an eye for a pretty woman, and he still liked to go on the odd binge as if to prove to himself that alcohol hadn't got the better of him. He joked, laughed, retailed old and new stories, read film scripts, and remained the nomad he was at that time. Someone summed up, 'He talks fast, the odd word with a soft Irish lilt. He is still youthful, rather serious, friendly, and less aggressive than one expected.'

With more songs and albums to come, his life was extremely busy. He slept little. As Lord of Tower House, he assumed a new status, yet no one envisaged his going to Buckingham Palace to be awarded an OBE. It was unthinkable.

16 *'Acting is not enough'*

In the bare temple-like sitting-room of Tower House he wrote his songs by humming them into a tape-recorder. That autumn of 1971 was an exceptionally busy one for Harris. Having just finished a film, *Man in the Wilderness*, he was now able to concentrate on his music. He had a new LP and a single on the way, and he could look forward to dates on BBC's *Top of the Pops*.

'Acting is not enough,' he told Robert Ottoway of the *TV Times*. 'I need several creative outlets, and singing, especially if you've written the songs yourself, is a great form of expression. Then, of course, there are poems. I was in New York recently. I had been invited to read some of my poetry to the Poetry Society. It gave me the greatest creative satisfaction I've ever had. Anyhow a few days later I went on a pub crawl, and *that's* what got into the papers. They'd conveniently forgotten about the poetry reading.'

Displaying amazing energy, he talked about the novel which he was writing called *Flanney at 1.10*; not everyone took him seriously about this literary venture because of the theme. 'It's all about a man who refuses to be born,' explained the actor. 'He'd rather spend his life in his mother's womb, with a butler to look after him, rather than face the outside world. I know it sounds strange, but I find myself totally absorbed.'

On the day that Clive Hirschhorn of the *Sunday Express* visited Harris he was tense and sober, shut away in his sitting-room in Tower House working with Phil Coulter on song arrangements. 'Jenny,' he shouted to his secretary, 'bring up my lyrics. They're in the kitchen.'

Coulter, like Jim Webb, was beginning to influence his music world. He had already won international recognition as a songwriter with 'Puppet on a String', which Sandi Shaw sang successfully at the Eurovision Song Contest in 1967; a year later his 'Congratulations' almost won the same contest for Cliff Richards. A perfectionist where music was concerned, Coulter found Harris dedicated to his music career and extremely professional. 'I began to enjoy working with Richard,' he said, 'not only on a musical basis but as an individual. We quickly established a working rapport.'

Already they planned a concert tour together throughout Britain, with Coulter conducting his own 30-piece orchestra. The Harris performance would last for more than two hours, with live sketches, songs and clips from his films and TV recordings. The songwriter admitted that one-night stands were gruelling, so was it for the money? Coulter said, 'Richard is probably a millionaire. From "Puppet" alone I've made tens of thousands of pounds. No, it's simply the challenge. Richard and I have never done anything like this before. We want to see if we can do it. It's a very exciting venture.'

Clearly, Harris was taking his singing seriously. His first record 'MacArthur Park' had by now sold a phenomenal five million copies. When not humming songs into his tape-recorder, he was in a West End recording studio putting together an album tracing the story of a man from his initial boy-meets-girl relationship through various landmarks of love and marriage. One of the numbers which he had written, 'All the Broken Children', concerned the break-up of a marriage and its effect on the children. His own three sons were still an important part of his life, and his own divorce, while traumatic, had not lessened his affection for them.

Early in October, his latest single 'My Boy' was released. It was a hit when he sang it on *Top of the Pops*, and it promised to reinforce the impact he had made three years previously with 'MacArthur's Park'. It prompted him to say, 'Singing doesn't come second after acting with me. If I wake up in the morning and have a great idea for a film, it takes six months at least to get the thing off the ground. By that time, I'm likely to be bored with it. Now if it's an idea for a song, I call up a songwriter or a producer, get into the studio, and a week later we've got the finished product.'

Musically, he had had a proud track record since 1968. In that year he had six records in the charts in the States and two gold discs. Although he didn't touch alcohol when he was working, there was a danger that he was pushing himself too hard and friends appealed to him to slow the pace. Harris was aware that he was becoming a workaholic, but he did find time for a drinking binge to relax himself between films and recording.

'I have worked so hard lately that I'm beginning to interfere with my way of life!' he joked. Could he possibly keep it up at forty-one? 'What really distresses me is that the hangovers are taking longer to disappear,' he admitted. 'That is probably a condition of age. Hangovers are like Dante's Inferno. It is like walking across the hot coals of Hell!'

By now he had installed a household staff in Tower House. As Phil Coulter hammered on the piano in the sitting-room, Harris paced the floor and tried out new songs. When the session was over he slumped on a window seat overlooking the garden and talked with feeling about his work. 'Why Did You Leave Me?', his own song, seemed to bring out the sensitive side of the actor. Although he did not read music or play any instrument, he had an instinctive feeling for music.

Journalists came away from Tower House intrigued by its eccentric occupant. 'Richard Harris gives the impression of being permanently engaged in guerrilla warfare,' commented one seasoned columnist. 'His mansion looks like the castle retreat of an active crusading knight. There he invites maidens, builds up the monumental hangovers and goes out for occasional battle.' He might have added that the actor also worked long hours there humming songs into a tape-recorder, writing poetry and reading scripts hurriedly dispatched to him by his agent.

The truth was that columnists never knew when the star was having them on. He was still a prankster at heart. For some women journalists in search of a colourful tale, Harris spun some gorgeous yarns. Invariably they transmitted them to their readers. Like the occasion he talked for the first time about the ghosts of Tower House. Trying to be serious, he told Ann Bayler of the *Daily Mail*, 'When I first bought the house eighteen months ago, I was scared out of my wits. I would hear a child crying in the loft, the piano playing in the lounge, footsteps on the minstrel gallery … Then one night I was in bed with a girlfriend when we heard the bedroom door open, and standing there in the frame of the door was the apparition of a woman. My girlfriend was terrified and I leaped out of bed and dashed across the room. But the apparition melted into thin air.

'Now I wouldn't be without my ghosts. I've grown used to them. If ever a girlfriend moves into the house and I want to kick her out all I have to do is phone and say I won't be home for the night. You'd be surprised how fast they pack their bags and get out.'

Despite his pranks and weird stories, he was essentially a realist. For someone who at that time had the image of a playboy, he achieved an enormous amount of work. His first volume of poetry was due for publication in the New Year, films were on the way, and cabaret in the New Year in America. Phil Coulter, who was an energetic worker, acknowledged that Harris's stamina was exceptional. The actor summed up, 'There's more to life than wine, women and brawls.'

In January 1972 his concert tour with the Coulter Orchestra aroused a good deal of publicity. For months the two Irishmen rehearsed the show, yet Harris was nervous about it, mainly because it was something entirely new for him and it was also quite a while since he had appeared before a live audience. With his painstaking approach, Coulter encouraged him and tried to iron out some music difficulties.

'I don't just want to sing a few songs, and call that an evening's entertainment,' Harris said. 'I think audiences will expect and deserve something a bit different. If they even just want me to talk, I'll be only too happy to oblige.' After his success in *Camelot*, it was confidently felt that his name would be enough to carry the show. It was also true that he faced a formidable array of critics who would probably be judging him on the same level as Sammy Davis Junior and Frank Sinatra.

As the opening night approached, he grew more nervous. 'I'm scared bloody stiff,' he said. 'They'll literally have to push me up the steps to get on. But it's something I want to do. If you really want to communicate with a live audience you can't do it on Broadway and certainly not in Shaftesbury Avenue. The people with heads, the thinking people, have gone from the theatre and they are going to concerts now.'

The tour got a mixed reception. Although never afraid of failure, Harris probably expected a more enthusiastic response from audiences. One particular critic, Robin Denselow, did not spare him and wondered what 'Richard Harris thought he was trying to do' and he rather doubted 'whether he knew himself'. He asked:

> Is it conceit or sheer self-deception? Why should a first-rate actor parade himself like a shambling tenth-rate Sinatra? True, he has handled a musical successfully, and gone on to record a series of albums, but when it comes to a full solo concert, there is no hiding behind a name or studio techniques. He tried to play it straight and just couldn't do it: the lights dimmed to a flickering clip from *Camelot*, up went the screen to reveal an orchestra, and Harris wandered on, dinner jacketed and hand in pocket, and launched straight into a batch of sentimental standards from 'How to Handle a Woman' to 'What Now My Love'. If it hadn't been him the audience, in my view, would have left within ten minutes.

The critic conceded that Harris had stage personality while singing, but he had little idea of vocal texture.

> The Harris myth of the glossy record sleeves collapsed fast, but then for a few minutes, a more real Harris was allowed to look in, telling Irish bar jokes and stories showing mistakes from his films, and putting on a delightfully funny cabaret turn.

Some critics suggested that the show was more suited to a nightclub atmosphere and that it did not fit easily into theatres. They saw enough to remind them that Harris had real potential as a cabaret artist, although he would have to work very hard on selecting his material. To Harris, it simply represented a challenge and he really had nothing to lose. He could afford at that time to experiment and he was said to be happy with most aspects of his own performance. He agreed, though, that cabaret was probably his scene.

Phil Coulter was philosophical about the tour. He thought that 'travelling' with Harris was often hilarious and he enjoyed the experience. He would not be drawn further.

Harris did not dwell for long on the vagaries of the tour, instead he jetted off to America where he had been booked for two nightly cabaret dates in New Orleans. Again the critics weren't sure of what to make of him. One said he couldn't sing for the life of him; another described him as the greatest entertainer that New Orleans had seen in the last decade. Either way, it seemed that he wasn't put out.

'I have my good nights and my bad nights,' he admitted. 'It doesn't worry me because I know it doesn't upset my kind of audience.'

He told them stories, recited his poems and sang love songs to them. American audiences appreciated his kind of showmanship better it seemed than their more sedate English counterparts. For Harris it was a celebration. He resented sleep, for he claimed it stole his 'precious time'. He loved the night and all of its intrigue.

'I'm always out to break more records by pushing my mind, body and spirit beyond the boundaries of normal human endurance,' he told a journalist at the Fairmont Roosevelt Hotel. In a torrent of words, he talked about his philosophy of life, his successes and failures.

'The other week in Dallas,' Harris mused, 'a woman came over to me and said, "I can count the number of times I've been to bed with you." I looked at her, because I never forget a face and I said, "Just when and where did it happen?" The lady shook her head and said, "Oh, no, not really ... but I always imagine it ... that you've been right there beside me in bed!" You see, my bones are clothed in celluloid. When my image dies so will all my fantasies.'

In New Orleans he stayed up late listening to jazz. He was the most important late-night guest of the Maison Bourbon and announced above the music that he was 'a nocturnal, nomadic person'. He said he rated Peter O'Toole as the greatest actor and Glenda Jackson as the best English actress. When he was asked when the hellraising was going to end, he shrugged his broad shoulders and looked towards heaven. 'One day it will,' he told his listeners in the Maison Bourbon. 'It's inevitable. There'll come a moment when I'll be walking down the street and some guy will say, "Hey, weren't you Richard Harris?" Then I'll know that Richard Harris was someone that people fictionalized. A man who was a fantasy in other people's dull and dour lives. I'll be ready to accept it, because I've done so many things in my life and accumulated so many experiences that it won't make any difference to me.

'I'll go on as long as I'm capable of going on. Although I'm forty-two I feel marvellous, full of vigour. I plan to continue my life as it is, regardless of criticism and regardless of accolades.'

Inevitably, his name was linked to women on both sides of the Atlantic, and on numerous occasions he was asked to describe his 'ideal woman'. It was becoming tiresome and some experienced women journalists reckoned it was a subject to be avoided, for Harris seemed to change his mind every week. When one young journalist unwisely asked the question, she was told by the star, 'My ideal woman is a beautiful, mute nymphomaniac who runs the local boozer.'

In some of his utterances about women he could be mocking, even cruel. He boasted, 'I never needed a woman to heal my wounds.' It was true up to a point. He considered that beds were made for bodies, not for souls. And: 'Girls just can't get the hang of doing things for pleasure. It's as if they've all been brought up in a puritan climate, where everything enjoyable is necessarily sin, so they have to assure themselves that they are wanted for their inner selves. And who wants to eat the core of an apple all the time?'

Friends hoped that he would soon settle down again and become less of a nomad. But there appeared at that time no woman in sight capable of taming the impulsive actor. He found time to make his New York concert début at the Philharmonic Hall in Lincoln Centre, and made an impression not only on audiences but on some critics. He announced that he was completing a selection of poetry to be published in the following year, 1973.

Eventually, when the book was published it bore the unusual title, *I, In the Membership of My Days* and Harris promoted it on both sides of the Atlantic. It was a nostalgic look at his life up to then, with poems about the wonder of romance and the joys of friendship. The poems reflected the lyricism and richness of the author's native Ireland.

There was no doubt that the book revealed once more the sensitive side to the actor as he recalled his childhood in Limerick, and the deaths of his parents and the sister closest to him, Harriet-Mary. He recalled such episodes as running away briefly from home, playing rugby in 'Our Lane' and imagining he was captaining Ireland against England in rugby football, and memories of the greenhouse at their home Overdale.

It was difficult to imagine that these poems, so full of meaning and pathos, came from a man who swept glasses off a bar counter in a brawl, or invited someone out to fight, to settle a dispute. A contradiction, perhaps, yet no one cared, especially those who appreciated the eccentricities of artists. When he was interviewed by Eamonn Andrews on a midday TV programme, he was annoyed that the presenter did not seem to take him seriously as a poet. 'I couldn't understand his attitude,' Harris recalls. 'In America they listened to me read my poetry and applauded me.'

Soon he would be forgetting for a while about writing poetry. One day while filming in Hollywood he met Ann Turkel, tall, slender and beautiful. She was middle-class and Jewish and was from Scarsdale, New York, and she made an immediate impression on Harris who was eighteen years her senior.

He had gone there to star in a spoof on 1940s gangster movies with the bizarre title of *99 and 44/100 per cent dead*. Jacqueline Bisset had turned down the co-starring role. When it was offered to Miss Turkel it made Harris wince. 'You're not going to wean an unknown actress,' he protested.

At that stage he was unaware that Ann was a fully fledged actress who had gained an arts theatre degree at Boston University. It was not long before he agreed that she had potential as an actress. 'I think she's going to be very good,' he confided in colleagues in Hollywood. As the days passed, they saw more of each other; she did not seem to be frightened by his rather fearsome reputation.

'There he was,' she said, 'my total opposite – a guy from Ireland, a hellraiser and brawler. More than that he was much older than me.' She swears that he didn't make a pass at her. At that time she was engaged to David Niven Jr. Soon she and Harris became lovers. 'We fell in love before we'd ever gone to bed with each other,' Ann says.

Her friends warned her about his wild past, how other women had discovered he was unmanageable. 'I didn't listen to them,' she recalls. 'I fell passionately in love with him.' She felt that in time she could tame the wayward Irishman. They became more than lovers, they were great pals and inseparable. She discovered another side to his complex nature – a man who was romantic, sentimental, patriotic, a gentle lover. She admitted that she became obsessed with him.

The romance became the talk of Hollywood. Harris began to

call her 'Turkey' in public. To the actor, it was a more affectionate name than Ann. In the middle of an interview he could be seen to hug her, and say, 'Turkey, you're bloody beautiful. I guess you've got me.' Others weren't so sure. They saw the liaison as another one of his fleeting romances; in a word, potentially disastrous for Ann.

Neither the gossip, nor the gossip columnists, worried her. 'If I believed all the wild stories I wouldn't be going out with Richard,' she said. 'Besides, there's no need to tame him; he is more of a lamb than a lion.' In subsequent months, he kept nothing from her. He revealed his past, warts and all; he didn't disguise the fact that he still talked to Elizabeth and that his children meant a great deal to him.

'What has gone before doesn't worry me,' Ann assured her friends. 'It's the future that counts. I've heard about his boozing, but he tells me he has got it under control. My folks in New York love Richard.'

A few of her close friends weren't convinced that Harris was converted to a conventional way of life. They reckoned that Ann was taking the biggest gamble of her career. 'Think about it, honey,' warned an ex-New York school friend. 'The guy's impossible.'

But she assured the press that she too had a past. She was careful to add, though, 'I've had some pretty good times. The only difference is that my relationships were important to me. I was first in love with an American boy. Then I fell for a Frenchman and, of course, over the past three years I have been with David Niven Jr. In the case of Richard, I hear about all those women who are supposed to have passed through his life. They were one-night affairs which had no meaning.'

She described her parents as 'broad-minded' and that they wouldn't object to her living with Richard provided they were sure he was going to marry her. It was important for her to live with a man to get to know him better. After a few months, she was able to say, 'I absolutely know we are made for each other.' At the time it sounded a hasty judgment on her part, even naïve.

Harris would not be drawn about marriage to Ann. It was one area in which he showed unusual caution. But it was soon obvious to colleagues on both sides of the Atlantic that in Ann Turkel he had met a strong-willed and a determined young woman who would not be easily intimidated by his talk of ghosts at Tower House. And he was the first to acknowledge she was different from most of the other women he had met.

17 'Fallon is the champion'

In the autumn of 1989, Richard Lester was directing *Get Back*, a new film starring Paul McCartney, at Twickenham Studios. Years before, he had directed *A Hard Day's Night* and *Help!*, both of which featured the Beatles. 'It was a privilege for me to be part of that era,' he says today.

In the mid-1970s he had directed Richard Harris in two movies, *Juggernaut* and *Robin and Marian*; in the latter Sean Connery and Audrey Hepburn were Harris's co-stars. Lester had also seen the actor's stage plays, but in retrospect it was *This Sporting Life* that made the biggest impression on him.

'It was, after all, the first film in which Richard starred,' he recalls, 'and to me it was a splendid screen début. He was also impressive in *Major Dundee* and, of course, *The Molly Maguires*.'

Lester took over the direction of *Juggernaut* at short notice after two previous directors (Bryan Forbes and Don Taylor) had been sacked. 'Richard Lester has the capacity of making a film your friend,' wrote one critic.

Until the mid-Seventies he had not met Harris. But he was aware of his reputation. Unlike some other directors who admitted they were scared of the wild stories, Lester was philosophical. 'I looked at it this way,' he remembers. 'I decided to wait and see how he treated me on the set. Really, I wasn't worried about the image built up around him.'

When he came to direct *Juggernaut* in 1975, he supplemented the existing line-up of Harris, Omar Sharif and David Hemmings with a distinguished cast that included Anthony Hopkins, Ian Holm, Shirley Knight, Roy Kinnear, Harris's old mentor Cyril Cusack, and Freddie Jones.

The story of the movie centres round the liner *Britannic*. Bombs are put aboard and before this is discovered she is at sea. A ransom is demanded ashore by a mysterious unseen terrorist whose code-name is Juggernaut. While the authorities on shore negotiate with the unknown figure, two bomb disposal experts are landed on the ship in a bid to defuse the explosives. At the same time police in London search frantically for Juggernaut.

As Fallon, one of the bomb disposal experts, Harris was playing one of his best screen parts in years. Fallon is an expert technician, a self-deprecating and humorous professional who, in a very short space of time, must save the ship in peril. His definition of death is that it is 'Nature's way of telling you you're in the wrong job'.

For the film, a Russian cruiser was hired by the company and sailed for Scotland with the stars and 280 'extras' on board. Shooting would begin when the bad weather came, but Richard Lester is a fast worker and the shooting was finished in eighteen weeks. 'I had no trouble with Richard Harris,' he recalls. 'He got on with the job and that suited me fine. His attitude for the part was just right.'

Stars had noted in the past that Lester worked faster than most directors. 'That is the way I like it,' he says. 'I know that, for instance, Richard Harris likes directors to finish a movie as quickly as possible. He hates boredom on location. We share that in common.'

Anthony Hopkins, who played Superintendent McCleod, agreed that he had never worked with as swift a director as Lester. As he said, 'Smash-bang. Four cameras and you're finished in about a week. The actors would meet on the set. "Stand by, action." He'd do one take, then say to us, "Right, do you want to do another?" "No," we'd say. "Okay, on we go." He was an incredibly fast worker and very pleasant too. I don't know whether it necessarily produces good results but it certainly pleases the producers.'

Although he described the part of Fallon as 'taut and tense', Lester was not sure that it was the best part that Harris played on screen. 'I don't think I could say that. Richard did, after all, play some other splendid roles, so one cannot be categorical. What I can say is that I enjoyed working with him. He caused me no worry at all. I am a fan of his, you know!'

After the sea-going sequences in *Juggernaut* were completed, Lester returned to Twickenham Studios where the remainder of the shoot, including scenes with the supporting cast were made.

Later, the movie was well received by the critics.

The film's ending is notably quiet and restrained. The relief of the passengers is muted because they have remained locked in their own isolation and therefore cannot share their feelings of relief. Fallon comes out on deck, but he is not congratulated for no one knows him or what he has done, and the camera pulls away, losing Fallon in the crowd, leaving us with the ship, moving slowly, uncertainly forward.

At the end though, Fallon is the champion, for his bomb-disposal skills have saved the passengers. To Harris, the role of Fallon was rewarding and his performance was praised by the critics. He was especially thinking of the final scene involving himself and Buckland, a disaffected former colleague who had planted the bomb (Freddy Jones), which is unbearably tense. As he hears the dancing on the upper deck of the ship while working to defuse the bomb, Fallon comments wryly, 'Civilization must be saved.'

Later in the scene, he asks Buckland, 'Is it the red or the blue wire?'

'Cut the blue wire,' says Buckland. After an agonizing moment in which Fallon debates within his own mind, he chooses to cut the red wire – and the ship is saved.

In Anthony Hopkins's view, it was a vastly under-rated thriller and one of Harris's best-ever screen performances. 'He really carried it off superbly,' he says.

Curiously, Harris does not include *Juggernaut* among his best half-dozen movies. Perhaps he sees it as just another taut thriller, full of suspense, otherwise ordinary.

It was a view also expressed by Cyril Cusack. 'I agree it is full of suspense but I consider it quite ordinary.' He was portraying O'Neill, an Irish terrorist. Thirty years before, he had acted beside Harris in *Shake Hands with the Devil* at Ardmore Studios in Bray. 'Richard was now a star,' he recalls. 'He had proved himself in such movies as *This Sporting Life, Mutiny on the Bounty* and *Camelot*. I considered him ideal for the role of Fallon.'

There is a moving moment in *Juggernaut* when Superintendent McCleod visits O'Neill in prison in the hope that he might give him a few leads. O'Neill cynically replies, 'I really don't care who gets blown up.' He taps his head in a very significant gesture, and adds, 'It's all up here, you see. And that's where it stays.'

In spite of past denials that he would remarry, Harris announced his engagement to Ann Turkel early in 1974. Proudly he introduced her to his friends in London and even brought her to Ireland where she was photographed more often than any politician. They announced that they would marry in April of that year. In Ireland, they stayed at the Cashel Arms Hotel run by Harris's brother-in-law, Jack Donnelly. The star spent most of his time clad just in a football jersey and slacks, as though eager to project his sports image. 'I'm still in love with rugby football,' he told a young reporter. 'And I regret I wasn't capped for Ireland.'

Ann learned about his Irish background. He concealed nothing about his wild youth, nor the fact that he had a very happy childhood. Before they left for London she felt she had known him since he was seven. 'It was extraordinary,' she said later, 'he talked about his past as if it was only yesterday.'

After six months they were still, on her own admission, 'madly in love'. Although he was still drinking, it was not on a constant basis. Secretly she worried about his low alcohol tolerance, for after three or four drinks he would be tipsy. She admitted that his energy was amazing and that she couldn't keep up with him despite her own considerable stamina. He was generous with money. She did not drink but was crazy about clothes and he purchased some lovely pieces for her.

Harris had by now decided to sell Tower House. He was sorry to see it go, for as he joked, 'I had gotten used to the ghosts.' He was to make a profit of £200,000 on the deal and, on James Bond producer Kevin McClory's suggestion, he invested in a large, picturesque house in the Bahamas. It was no ordinary house. Situated on Paradise Isle, on one side is the boat dock, leading to a lush garden heady with the scent of bougainvillaea, and on the other side is a palm-fringed lawn running down to a sandy beach lipped by an impossibly blue ocean. Sharks are kept at bay by an obliging reef, a little way offshore.

The house with its screened porches, blue walls, peeling paintwork, white-shuttered windows and ten bedrooms,

November 1982 saw the return of *Camelot* to the London stage:
Fiona Fullerton as Queen Guinevere joins Harris's King Arthur at the
Apollo Victoria.

Airports – the thorn in the jet-setter's side. Harris pictured *en route* to New York in 1985, and (with Ann Turkel) eleven years earlier, prepares to make the same journey in order to promote his latest volume of poetry.

With ex-wife Elizabeth
in 1988.

A white-bearded Harris on the Connemara set of his latest movie, *The Field.* With him is playwright John B. Keane, whose work was adapted for the screen by Jim Sheridan.

Harris made a big hit with local children when he officially opened Connemara Sea Week – he is here pictured with Megan Vine of Clifden.

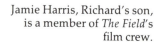

Jamie Harris, Richard's son, is a member of *The Field*'s film crew.

formerly belonged to the American millionaire Huntingdon Hartford (who also owned the entire island). All the main rooms open on to both sides of the house and a gentle breeze blows perpetually off the sea.

When asked to describe it, Ann liked to say, 'It is a lovely old house, faintly dilapidated, built on a spit at the end of the island.' She decided to decorate it herself. Harris was used to deriding the sort of houses in which movie stars usually lived. His preference was for simplicity and comfort. He was able to say at last that he had discovered his dream house – and dream island.

They were not long living there, when he invited a friend, writer Don Short, to view the house. 'Come on over!' he proclaimed. 'We're having one hell of a honeymoon!'

'Honeymoon!' exclaimed the other. 'I thought the wedding was not until April ... or are you already married to Ann?'

Harris roared with laughter.

'No, no,' he asserted. 'We're having the honeymoon first because there'll not be time for such luxuries after the wedding. We're both committed to work in the same week.'

'Are you sure I won't be in the way?'

More laughter from Harris.

'Not at all,' he assured his friend. 'As long as your foot doesn't tread the bedroom stairs.'

'Okay,' said his friend. 'I'll see you at your love nest.'

Originally, the wedding was planned to take place on 7 April, but it was 'unavoidably' postponed. The excuse given for the postponement was that the pair were not fully prepared. Someone else claimed they had quarrelled. Harris, however, assured the world that he had been too busy completing movies and it would have to wait until June.

This time there were no hitches. They were married at Beverly Hills, with Ann looking more radiant than ever. A three-week honeymoon was planned.

They spent it in the idyllic surroundings of the Bahamas. To the surprise of visitors, he announced he wanted to get to know Ann better. 'Until now I've seen her only for a few minutes in the mornings before I go filming,' he said. 'Then for a few minutes in the evening, before I go to the recording studios. And for a few hours between, in working lulls.'

He was determined to take a few months off to relax. Slyly, he said, 'We'll see how we get on being in each other's pockets twenty-four hours a day. Who knows? It might turn out to be a case of bed and bored.'

Sometimes Ann preferred to leave the talking to her husband. It pleased Harris enormously. 'That's the marvellous thing about beautiful women,' he mused, 'they're always getting their coiffure coiffured, legs waxed and all that jazz. It gets them out of your hair for an hour.'

Sometimes he liked his own company without any other intrusion. At such times he'd sleep, wake up and read, or perhaps write a few lines of poetry. It was something that Ann Turkel began to notice and then she would be careful to go her own way for a while, knowing that he cherished those little moments to himself. The solitude brought him calm, even serenity.

When he was asked why, in this permissive age, he had bothered getting married to Ann, he said quietly, 'Ann's a well-brought up girl ... whatever that means. She's also very nice and talented. I've made no bones that I'm not good news for any girl. I told her father, "If I was in your place I'd have a contract out for Harris's head in five minutes." All he did was to laugh. But as it was a phone conversation, I couldn't see if it was through gritted teeth. There were no other reasons why I thought it was a good idea to get married.'

Ann told friends that she wanted a child by Richard. Harris said, 'I'd like a daughter. I've already got three sons.'

It was perhaps ironic that, at a time when he was renewing himself and finding a new surge of happiness, his ex-wife Elizabeth was unhappily married to Rex Harrison. As she recalled, 'I knew now that our days were numbered. Sometimes Rex recognized it, and sometimes he didn't. It was uncanny how after a blazing row, he could pick up the telephone and talk to me as if the whole thing had never happened. We were now spending more time apart than together.'

Harris had by now introduced Ann to his three sons and intended having them for holidays on his Paradise island. Nor had he entirely forgotten their mother, Elizabeth. He knew that her marriage wasn't working out – and wasn't altogether surprised.

*

At that time it had come to his notice that Oliver Reed was making rude remarks about him. Although he did not take Reed seriously, neither did he ignore him. In the past he refused to comment to the press on such occasions and simply described Reed as 'a bore' and said he could not understand why he talked about him.

'Oliver Reed did three films that I turned down,' he explained, 'so he should be extremely grateful to me.' He admitted, though, that he once sent the actor a pair of crutches with two names engraved on them; one Ken Russell, the other, Glenda Jackson. The implication was that Reed would fall without their support.

Reed, who was ten years younger than Harris, was irked. He began to describe himself as Mr England, and to take 'digs' at Harris. The latter's reaction was as unpredictable as it was amusing. He sent Reed a book of his poems with a note on the fly-leaf: 'To Oliver – Mr England. Since you have not yet attained superstar status and salary and therefore cannot afford to buy this book, here is a copy free.' It was signed 'Richard – Mr Ireland'. And there was a postscript which read, 'You are the only person I know who would go out of his way to claim an affinity with a bankrupt nation.'

In time, Reed who often did more outrageous things than Harris, realized that members of the Hellraisers Club, to which he steadfastly belonged, had their own code of conduct and could indulge in friendly rivalry. As he said, 'Harris often made outrageous statements about me to reporters, but we were both sensible and professional enough to know they were manufactured entirely for the benefit of the press. Just as he realized it was all part of the game when I phoned the Hollywood gossip writers and threatened to sue them and Richard Harris for the things he had said and they had printed about me. But some of the papers would get the wind up and offer to apologize.'

Nonetheless, Reed's press quotes were carefully worked on and ensured at that time that he made the headlines. Once, he was quoted as saying,

Lee Marvin is the roughest, toughest movie star in the business – and the hardest drinker. He'd make Richard Harris look like a half pint of stale Guinness and Dean Martin like a wet Martini.

The funny thing was that Harris and Reed had never actually met, though the latter once wrote,

> We did once when I was a young extra which he won't remember. It was when I had a small part in a TV series. I was working at Elstree and sought out my friend, Ronnie Fraser, who had a part in another production being shot at the same studio. I knocked on Ronnie's dressing-room and Harris came to the door. He snarled, 'What do you want?' I asked if Ronnie Fraser was there. He said 'Yes, he is,' and slammed the door in my face. But I don't hold a grudge against him for that. I was a nobody then and he was a big star.

Harris and Peter O'Toole were on amiable speaking terms and occasionally attended one another's stage performances. Driving through London with a friend on the night of the première of *Laurence of Arabia*, Harris looked at his watch and remarked good-humouredly, 'In fifteen minutes' time O'Toole's era of anonymity will be over.'

In a jokey moment, O'Toole, who was by then slowing up as a hellraiser, described Harris as 'that Limerick lout', but it was to a friend and not to the actor's face. There was a friendly rivalry between them and they liked to think they viewed the world through the same broad lenses. In a way their careers ran on parallel lines. Both, like Richard Burton, had started out with a passion for the theatre and later graduated to films. They had no answer to the charge that they deserted the stage for a more lucrative career in films, although O'Toole once replied, 'Films and stage – it's all acting. Fortunately I can choose what I want to do.'

It was claimed that Harris's neglect of the stage was more serious than O'Toole's. Colleagues expected him to play a season or two of Shakespeare at Stratford-on-Avon, believing it would advance his acting career; instead, he became a nomadic actor between one global film set and the next. Arguably, because he was a big spender, he needed the money, yet his friends were disappointed by his decision.

Now, in the mid-1970s he showed no great inclination to return to the stage; he was content with accepting more film roles and with his reputation growing there was no shortage of offers. Creativity was what mattered to him. It was the only thing that gave him complete fulfilment. Acting alone seemed to him an empty occupation, with its lengthy hours of idleness.

Despite a full schedule, he still found time for diversions. He reckoned they were necessary to keep his adrenalin flowing. Once he received a telegram from Oliver Reed that he (Reed) had to go to bed with Racquel Welch in the movie *The Prince and the Pauper* and offering him a job as a stand-in, providing his wig didn't fall off in the clinches. 'I was always sending Harris telegrams like that,' recalls Reed, 'and receiving quite a few from him in similar vein.'

To Harris, characters like Oliver Reed and himself were necessary to enliven the business, and to keep one's perspectives right. He thought that some actors took their careers too seriously; others believed the publicity written about them. He himself preferred to strike a happy balance.

18   *The African connection*

When Burt Lancaster was unavailable to play the role of Rafer Janders in *The Wild Geese*, it was offered to Harris and he accepted without hesitation. He made no secret of the fact that he welcomed the opportunity of joining Richard Burton in South Africa.

Burton was cast as Colonel Allen Faulkner, leader of the mercenaries. 'The part is tailor-made for me,' he said. Producer Euan Lloyd had read the book in proof and decided that with its story of a group of mercenaries hired by an influential banker, Sir Edward Matherson, to rescue the kidnapped leader of a small African state, it was exciting movie material, and he immediately set about securing the rights to make a film based on the novel.

In the autumn of 1977, Harris travelled with his wife Ann to join the rest of the cast before they set out for the tiny health spa of Tschipse, in South Africa, just below the Rhodesian border. The town, once a stopping station between Salisbury and Johannesburg, had developed into a very popular holiday resort, built around the mineral baths there.

Director Andrew McLaglen reckoned it was the perfect location for *The Wild Geese*. With modern facilities in the spa town, a bracing climate, and good surrounding terrain, the cast looked forward to a fruitful time. Producer Euan Lloyd admitted that there was surprise in the industry when it was announced that he had cast Harris and Burton together in the movie. He knew that both enjoyed a reputation for wildness, but it was also generally accepted that their 'wildest days' were drawing to an end.

'The situation was not as explosive as it looked,' said Lloyd. 'I knew that both Harris and Burton were extremely professional actors and, despite their reputations, were always dry when working. Furthermore, they would not be drinking alcohol while in Africa. I was aware that both men had been warned off drink by their doctors, so really I had no fears.'

At that time, Harris said, 'The crazy period of my life is over. I really enjoyed it and have no regrets. But I have a different approach to life now. Before, I always had public excitements which the public loved to read about. Today my excitements are private. They are strictly between me and my wife, Ann. They are not for the world any more. The world can go and screw itself.'

In the previous months he had been relatively sober. He said he felt like thirty since he went on the wagon. 'You see,' he mused, 'my wife Annie is already a good influence on me.' He liked to call her Annie.

However, she admitted that she was terrified of him when he drank too much. She hated to see him lose his temper and get involved in drunken brawls. It was too soon, she knew, to predict whether he would stay on the wagon for long. Co-starring with Burton and Roger Moore, and playing a mercenary commando, posed a challenge for him. For a long time he had admired Burton and now he found they could converse easily together and joke about their wild times. 'Christ, we're both damn lucky to be alive, you know,' Burton declared.

Now they shared something else in common, apart from starring together in the movie. They were desperately trying to remain on the dry. Harris made no secret of the fact, nor did Burton.

'When I saw Richard on the set,' recalls Harris, 'he was trying to stay off drink. He was really terrific, marvellous. The courage of that guy. But there was agony and pain in his abstinence. I thought well, I'm beyond that stage. I was as bad as him in 1970, so why carry on and get that way again? I had myself tested and my insides were fine. I was ahead of the game, so I eased up.'

Together, under the African sun, they discussed their turbulent lives, as if they were brothers. It was a stimulating moment for Harris, for he sensed that Burton wanted to look into himself, to retrace the tortuous road he had walked.

One day, Burton asked him, 'Richard, what was the worst part of your past?'

The question took Harris by surprise. He thought for a moment, then said, 'What I can't remember and what other people enjoyed.'

The frankness of the answer amused Burton and instantly triggered off a similar line of thought in his own mind. He agreed with a faint smile that there were many 'lost moments' in his own life, too.

Burton remembered previously meeting him three times, but Harris could only recall one of those times. As he said, 'The stories he tells about the other two meetings are hilarious and totally unprintable.'

It was the stifling African heat that Andrew McLaglen found most hard to take. However, watching the two Richards, Harris and Burton, cure their thirsts with pints of water amused him no end. 'It was funny seeing these two old hellraisers off the booze and not complaining. I guess the iced water kept them both off the hard stuff. Of course I was aware of their reputations when I came to make the movie, but I lost no sleep over that. They gave me no trouble.'

To McLaglen, the most abiding memory was the camaraderie between the two actors and Roger Moore. He never failed to be astonished by their friendship. Since both Harris and Burton wanted to be called Richard, he decided to call Burton, Richard I, and Harris, Richard 2. That ended the confusion that arose at the start of the movie.

The director, a son of the veteran Hollywood star, Victor McLaglen, found that the two stars did not spare themselves, despite the intense heat. He reckoned that *The Wild Geese* was one of Burton's better movies in the latter part of his career.

The stars' wives, Ann Harris, Susie Burton and Luisa Moore were enjoying their African experience. Roger and Luisa Moore were able to enjoy Martinis together in the evenings, but the two other couples were more abstemious. 'It was amazing how well the wives got on,' recalls Harris. 'I could see that Annie enjoyed watching us make the movie.'

It amused him once to find his wife and Susie Burton sitting nearby discussing their husbands and the demon booze. The women both agreed that the two Richards had been boring drunks. 'I can accept that now,' Harris says today, 'but I would never have dreamt I was a boring drunk at the time.'

The Wild Geese was, on his own admission, the happiest film he ever made. 'Honestly, we were like a crazy band of schoolboys. It brought out the child in us. I told Richard Burton one day, "I've made this film before. When I was in Limerick as a kid, I would always be daydreaming that I was off in Africa. Fighting people, saving my gang." And he said, "So was I. A little kid in Wales, always in the trees, with a machinegun." '

To Harris, it was an extraordinary feeling, as though he had gone back miraculously in time. Listening to the voice of Burton, with its soft Welsh lilt, made him feel relaxed. He later said, 'And there we were in South Africa, living in a dream. In a fantasy. We were like ten-year-olds playing in our backyards, having terrific fun.

'We would arrive in the morning dressed in our uniforms. OK, what game are we going to play today. It was wonderful Boys' Own stuff and we had such a wonderful time that we decided to come back again some time and do another movie.'

There was something about Richard Burton, says Ann Turkel, that appealed to her husband at that time. 'Richard had told me that he got on with Sean Connery because he was a man's man. It was different I believe with Richard Burton. It reminded me of two poets meeting one day and loving each other's poetry or paintings. I could see that Richard was enthusiastic about their conversations and wanted to talk for hours. Drink was not involved. They were happy chatting together, in the shade and out of the sun.'

It was a shrewd observation. To Burton, Harris was an unpredictable and genuine Celt, a man after his own heart. Both hated bullshit. Burton did not care a damn, for instance, that Harris had played King Arthur in the film of *Camelot*, which he, Burton, had made famous on the stage. 'The luck of the game,' he called it. In a way, both Richards were nomadic actors, at once restless and impulsive, seeking an impossible Utopia.

Harris loved to relive happier moments in his life. It was one of the reasons why he wanted to return to South Africa again, a vast and beautiful country, he described it. It was one of the reasons why he returned to Ireland every so often, and to the little County Clare resort of Kilkee to renew his childhood. It was important to him, a kind of reassurance that it wasn't all a dream.

The late 1970s were turning out to be a satisfying time in his life. Film offers kept coming in. Since he had stopped drinking, he found that his wife was much more relaxed and their lives had become absolutely blissful. 'We've got a super relationship. I like to be with her all the time. We are terrifically compatible, in that we are both excitement freaks. We both have the same impulses at the same moment. If we want to get up and go, we go. There are no greys in my life at all. Everything's either black or white. Either right at the peak or in the depths. There's no middle, we won't accept any middle. We are people of passion.'

Nonetheless, his wife remained apprehensive. While she adored her husband sober, she found it difficult to cope with his dark moods when he drank vodka or whisky. Whenever he said to her, 'Annie, I'm stopping drinking for life,' she replied, 'Ha-ha, I've heard that one before.'

The Wild Geese was a big box-office success in Britain and some other countries, but it failed to attract Americans in big numbers to make it a commercial success. Strangely, despite the fact that he got on extremely well with his co-stars Richard Burton and Roger Moore and considered the film dramatically convincing, Harris does not include it among his dozen best movies.

The appeal of Africa stayed with the Harrises, and they went on to make two more movies there, *Golden Rendezvous* and *A Game of Vultures*, in which Harris played the role of a sanctions-busting businessman in a guerrilla war, similar to the war that was raging at that time in Rhodesia.

It was while he was staying in Johannesburg that a scandal erupted around him and made him global news once more. In evidence before a Commission of Inquiry, film producer Andre Pieterse, said he had been given a loan of £460,000 from a secret South African government fund to save his film *Golden Rendezvous* from financial disaster. Pieterse originally got into trouble with *Golden Rendezvous* when it went more than £1 million over budget, and he had failed to sell the project – based on an Alister Maclean story – to American cinemas. He claimed that Richard Harris, star of the movie, had made it impossible for him to leave the set to arrange other finance because the actor had been drinking.

Harris was furious. 'I don't want to hurt the guy because I don't believe in kicking a man while he's down,' he said. 'The truth is that Pieterse found himself in trouble and is trying to hang people for it. I'm a perfect scapegoat. I live a very, very raucous flamboyant private life. Well, I used to.'

Confronted with a judge's order for Harris's arrest, the

producers of *A Game for Vultures* began to make plans to smuggle him out of the country. Hazel Adair, who wrote the script and was the co-producer of *Golden Rendezvous*, arranged to fly the star to the Indian Ocean island of Mauritius in one of the film's DCs.

'It was a very tricky moment,' said author Colin Mackenzie, Hazel's son who was on the point of flying to Africa to oversee the escape. 'My mother had nearly completed the film and said it was Richard's best performance in years.'

The threat of arrest receded when Harris – who was stated to be on the dry – issued a counter-claim against Pieterse for £14 million alleging defamation.

Harris, who would shortly celebrate a year of temperance recalls, 'I worked on that movie seven days a week, eighteen hours a day. Mr Pieterse asked me on four occasions to take over the direction. Would he ask that of someone incapable?'

At his hotel he later assured journalists that he had put his drinking days behind him. He was pictured in the papers with a glass of coke in one hand. More damaging to his career at this stage was the criticism being levelled against him for making poor movies. Listed among them were *The Wild Geese*, *A Game for Vultures* and *Gulliver's Travels*. Later, he would say, 'I went through a time when I didn't care what films I did – I just hired them my body and my voice.'

Funnily, at the time he enjoyed making the films and was in no way reluctant to discuss them with journalists. There was a new deep-sea film, *Orca – Killer Whale*, in which he played a fisherman engaged in a life-and-death struggle with a whale whose mate he had accidentally killed. Since he started work on *Orca – Killer Whale*, he had read exhaustively on the subject.

'Once,' he said, 'a fishing boat accidentally struck and wounded a female Orca. Just as in our film, her mate followed the boat, attacked and sank it. The crew had to take to the life rafts – but they were left unharmed. Killer whales are considered by seamen to be the most vicious and voracious of sea animals. But for about twelve years, captured killer whales (Orcas) have been trained to work in aquariums around the world. This is the measure of their intelligence, they're friendly to man, and perform for him once they've been trained.'

Harris's deep interest in the subjects of the films he accepted underlined his sense of professionalism and made a mockery of assertions that he 'jumped from film to film without bothering to study the script'.

When he accepted an offer, for instance, to star in the latest version of *Gulliver's Travels* he involved himself so deeply that it looked as though he were doing *Hamlet*. He lived for the excitement of the moment. In another way, it was the weirdest screen job he had ever been asked to do.

When he was rehearsing his conversations with the Lilliputians he spoke to model figures. Once the cameras rolled, these were removed. Aside from this whimsical dramatic exercise, Harris underwent unique physical discomfort. He lay for days on the studio floor being measured for the trolley and specially made miniature ropes and nails which the Lilliputians use when they take him prisoner. He remained in this immobile position under the burning studio lights while reciting his lines.

Production designer Michael Stringer says today, 'Richard must have gone through sheer agony, but he stuck it out to the end. He is patient and professional.'

It was Stringer's inspiration that helped to make this version of Swift's eighteenth-century classic into a pioneer work. Made at Pinewood and in Belgium, it was the first film combining humans, animated drawings and three-dimensional miniature sets. When Harris, as Gulliver, strides through Lilliput, he is really picking his way across a vast area of miniature models of houses and animals which covered the largest stage at Pinewood. When he captures the enemy armada he is really fulfilling a small boy's dream of wading across a pond with a whole fleet of toy boats.

'I spent six months making the film,' recalls Harris, 'and I am on the screen almost all of the time. It was a new challenge and I happen to like challenges.'

The African connection had made Ann Harris happy. The small roles she had played in some of her husband's films afforded her a sense of fulfilment. 'I fell in love with South Africa,' she said. 'I have beautiful memories of my days there.' It was clear that the Harrises were under scrutiny. Everyone wanted to know more about their tense and passionate relationship, and whether it was too explosive to last. Bart Mills in the *Guardian* observed:

Being a bully still occupies much of Richard Harris's time. Marriage has mellowed him, but it hasn't killed his restless urge to dominate, by charm or by force. Most people are happy to be dominated by such an exorbitantly talented and endlessly amusing man. He has to keep busy to repel all the would-be hangers-on who want nothing more than to sponge off his personality.

Mills revealed that the star had developed what he called 'his code of rudeness' to ensure that no one got too close to him. He was secure, direct, and he did what he wanted to do. Few people, Mills argued, had succeeded in penetrating Harris's off-putting exterior to find the baby within that's wailing. The actor told him, 'I'm sort of tutoring my wife. It's a very well thought out policy, you see. I give a lot of time now to guiding her acting career – tell her which movies to turn down. Mark me well, Ann Turkel will be playing leading parts very soon.'

For the most part, the *Guardian* columnist concentrated on Ann's career with reference to her amateur photography. During their interview, she showed him photographs of her husband, saying, 'No one makes him look as good as me. I shoot him from the heart.' Bart Mills found her a woman of quick enthusiasms whose moody tigress face lit up at the mere mention of Richard's name. She was unnaturally tall and lean, and enjoyed chauffering her husband around. And she wasn't jealous of his status as a star.

If nothing else, she was open and frank and the media found this facet of her character appealing. 'Richard and I share everything,' she said. 'He's my best friend. My psychiatrist. My pal, husband, lover, everything. No one knows what I know about him. He's such a little baby, and I take care of him.'

Since their marriage, she talked of taming him. She claimed he had been used to getting away with murder all his life, and he'd never had an equal. When they first married, she never talked back to him. Now she yelled at him. 'Sure we fight,' she said. 'Richard says Gable and Lombard had fights and so should we. There are no greys in my relationship with Richard. We have tremendous highs, and we have tremendous lows. We know even when we're fighting that afterwards the high is going to be great. We both live off excitement.'

It was the most revealing disclosure of the interview, and one of the reasons why friends of the pair wondered if at the end of the day the marriage would be able to survive the tremendous lows. It was deeper than that. In the last few years, Harris had found that as she had matured as a young woman she was demanding so much of him that it was threatening his career. He quit singing and he felt his acting was sliding. As he said, 'I didn't care about the script; the only thing that mattered was the size of the cheque.'

Being a fiercely independent spirit, he found that the balance was wrong. 'I was beginning to get sick of being part of her life rather than my own. I couldn't be bothered to keep acting out the parts she wanted me to play at home.'

Although Ann would deny it, he felt she was beginning to take him for granted, and as he said, he was too big a star to let that happen. Nonetheless, in between the clashes of temperament, they enjoyed happy times on Paradise Isle. But it was true that Ann was restless; she wanted her film career to take off, now that it seemed unlikely that they would have a child. 'Ann had wanted to have children ever since we got married,' Harris said. 'She was pregnant once, but had a miscarriage on a 747 plane at 32,000 ft and 600mph. After that we never really got round to it.'

At times, it seemed that the disparity in their ages was to blame for their latest rows. Harris was aware of this important factor in their marriage. 'When you marry a girl so much younger than yourself, you lose your identity in trying to be what they want you to be, and trying to keep up with them. It is very novel to begin with, but gradually it gets tiring. I soon found that I was mollifying my behaviour, tastes and outlook, just for her. I began to neglect a lot of things because of Ann, particularly my own career.'

If he was really talking freedom rather than independence, then his marriage to Ann seemed doomed. Not everyone was blaming the temperamental star for putting the marriage at risk. Ann was said to be quick-tempered and in her own way as fiery as her husband.

'She's far from demure,' wrote one American columnist. 'She once wrenched the door off the Beverly Hills hotel room in which Richard was sulking. It had often seemed that they find it hard to live with – or without – each other.'

There was already gossip of loud quarrels between the pair, at both their home in the Bahamas and in Beverly Hills. Soon their strained relationship became a talking point on Paradise Island when a judge ordered that the couple should try to bring about a reconciliation with a deadline set for September. Harris retorted, 'But I brought the action for incompatibility, so if Annie does not accept my conditions for complete independence, I'll see to it that the marriage is over in September.'

As ever, Harris seemed to take life's traumas in his stride. In America, he appeared in a cable television production of *Camelot* which received enthusiastic reviews. Said to be the most expensive programme of its kind ever made, the making was attended by fiery disagreements between Harris and the producer, culminating in the star's walking out and a shouting match in the street, with Harris bellowing at the producer, 'You want me to hit you, don't you?'

At a preview screening for the press in New York, he contrived to embarrass everyone present by prolonged slow clapping when the offending producer's name was mentioned. A television journalist in the audience pronounced his verdict on the cause of the trouble by ostentatiously tapping his glass of wine. The word that he had given up drinking had clearly not spread far.

Back in Paradise Island, Harris found the peace he sought. Living there seemed to bring out the ascetic side of the man. He wanted for nothing. Most days he got up at about eight o'clock, jogged on the beach and spent the morning reading or writing. He still talked vaguely about writing his autobiography wickedly entitled, *People I Did and People I Didn't.* 'It's going to be about some of the most wonderful people in the world I have met, and some of the biggest assholes.'

In the afternoons, when it got hot, he took a nap, and most evenings he watched videos of old films. He had to eat regularly, watch his diet and take a daunting number of pills to balance his blood sugar level. But he hadn't lost the art of storytelling and he liked nothing better than to dine with friends at a restaurant by the waterfront in Nassau and recall some of the hilarious court appearances he had made in his time. He embellished the stories by playing the prosecuting counsel and the judge himself, changing his facial expression for each part; at the end of it even the Bahamian waitress was shrieking with laughter.

The funny thing was that he didn't need alcohol to make him the best of company. Sober, his memory seemed superb, but it was the way he told the stories that captivated the other diners at his table. It reminded them perhaps that his *métier* in the theatre was comedy, and not the Shakespearean plays such as *Hamlet* and *King Lear* he so badly wanted to do. It was the light touch that Irish actor Godfrey Quigley first observed in him during his performance of *The Ginger Man* in Dublin. 'I think Dickie would be more remarkable in Coward than Shakespeare,' Quigley had predicted. 'His light touch is unsuited to tragedy.'

Friends, even colleagues, urged him to get back to the stage and forget those 'awful movies' he had been making. As he got back his full strength on his island home it seemed they had convinced him, for whenever film offers came along he studied them closely to ascertain whether they were worth thinking about.

Eventually, when that stage call arrived, it was as unexpected as it was attractive.

19   *A call from Los Angeles*

He had been filming in the jungles of Sri Lanka, playing Bo Derek's father in *Tarzan, the Apeman*, and was returning to his Paradise home in the Bahamas when he was offered *Camelot* – this time on stage.

To Harris, it was an agreeable surprise, something entirely out of the blue. The thought, however, of mounting again the throne of King Arthur made him feel apprehensive. Burton was a hard man to follow. As he explained, 'Here's a man who can just stand still on the stage and even if the other actors are eating the scenery he is still the one to watch.'

He had closely followed Burton's progress in the stage production. The tour had opened in June 1980. Prior to that, the show won rave notices in New York. As one critic said, 'Richard Burton remains every inch the King Arthur of our most majestic storybook dreams.' It didn't seem to matter that Clive Barnes, the formidably influential New York critic, had described him as 'a knight to forget'.

After New York *Camelot* played for two weeks in Chicago, three weeks in Dallas, four weeks in Miami Beach, three weeks in New Orleans and twelve weeks in San Francisco. Burton did not miss a single performance but on reaching Los Angeles, where the show was booked for a three-month run, he had soon to admit defeat. He dropped out of the production and into St John's Hospital, where he was told he needed major surgery on his spine.

Harris decided to accept the role of King Arthur, despite the prospect of a gruelling tour. In a generous gesture to his friend Richard Burton, he said, 'It's impossible to follow an act like Burton's, but I'll get along.' He remembered their memorable time together in South Africa making *The Wild Geese* and the truce they had drawn up not to drink. When Burton later heard that Harris had once broken the truce, he was heard to say, 'If I'd started drinking, I'd have made Africa burn.'

Although it had been some years since he had filmed *Camelot*, Harris was still familiar with the Lerner and Loewe score and could instantly hum numbers like 'If Ever I Would Leave You', 'The Lusty Month of May' and 'How To Handle a Woman'. And he simply loved the role of the tragic monarch, who forges a company of chivalrous knights only to see it splinter against the onslaught of jealousy and greed.

At that time, increasing criticism had been levelled against him for making worthless movies, in particular *Tarzan* which was reckoned a considerable climbdown from *The Wild Geese* and *This Sporting Life*. He argued it was 'all acting' and that he wouldn't have accepted the roles if he hadn't wanted to.

Similarly, Burton had been accused of going for the money at the expense of his talent. After making *The Wild Geese*, he had made movies for which producers had difficulty finding distributors. His more recent success in the stage version of *Camelot* had, however, given him an important new impetus and convinced him he had made mistakes in his career.

The musical looked also like revitalizing Harris's waning career which had lost any semblance of direction. Simply, he had been talking too much and, as an actor, doing too little of real stage or screen value. Living in luxury in the Bahamas seemed to have diminished his ambition; the old fire, once an integral part of his make-up, was no longer conspicuous; marriage with Ann had also taken up much of his time. Friends thought that a long stage run was just the fillip he needed to restore his vitality and appetite for the theatre.

It would be his first stage appearance in fifteen years; that fact alone tended to make him nervous. Frank Dunlop flew from London to work with him on the role of King Arthur. The star was reputed to be getting £25,000 a week plus a share of the profits to play the King. There was a buzz in Los Angeles on the eve of the opening in April 1981. Tickets were almost impossible to come by.

For the blue-eyed actor from Limerick, the evening was a triumph. Next day's reviews described him as better than Burton and credited him with having taken a theatrical corpse and, by the sheer force of his talent and charisma, making it once again a living thing.

The musical, one of the most expensive ever produced on America's West Coast, had opened more than a month before with Burton in the leading role. It ran to lukewarm reviews and mediocre houses. Harris's powerful impact as the king ensured that the show would have a lengthy run. 'It went better than I thought,' he reflected. 'I had been a long time away from the stage, and it takes time to get back the feel again.'

In the Los Angeles *Herald Examiner*, theatre critic Jack Viertel said that Harris attacked the role like a hungry dog who had been thrown a prime rib – he jumped on the part and devoured it.

'It is Harris's evening. He has pulled off an astonishing feat in stepping into Burton's shoes and delivering a performance that looks like it had months of thought and preparation poured into it.'

Furthermore, Viertel thought that the actor's emotional grip on the role was total, describing his performance as brilliant. 'In one case he has turned a hitherto meaningless musical number, "What Do Simple Folk Do", into a startlingly theatrical evocation of growing despair,' he stated. 'It is like the rest of his perform-ance, a brilliant reading of the possibilities inherent in the role.'

'Harris is freer and less grave than Burton, suiting many of the Lerner and Loewe songs better than the Welsh actor,' wrote the *Los Angeles Times* critic.

Harris was as much relieved as thrilled by his own successful comeback. It convinced him that the role of King Arthur was made for him and emphasized the regal elements that others saw in his stage presence. At fifty, it was important to his career to have a success; his stage confidence as an actor returned, ably assisted by the star treatment given him everywhere he went. It reminded him of the adulation after the screen success of *Camelot*. It was the nice part of show-business and he never ceased to revel in it, realizing at the same time that fame was ephemeral and he could not always hope to bask in such an intense glare. From the days when he first tasted stardom in *This Sporting Life*, he tended to celebrate late into the night on such occasions. As always, he was a night person.

In Los Angeles it was somewhat different. He talked a great deal, but drank little, mostly a glass or two of wine. He had been warned off alcohol by his doctors. Now, as friends and well-wishers crowded around his dressing-room, or dined with him late, he loved the feeling of excitement and camaraderie. He responded to excitement as though it were an inescapable part of the scene.

As the tour of America continued, it was noticeably taking its toll on him by the week. In the dressing-room after the show he would perspire profusely. 'I'm absolutely exhausted,' he would say, a vein in his temple standing out like a lightning flash against the pasty flesh. At his hotel he had a case of wine specially flown in from New York. It was a 1976 red Château Lafite Rothschild and cost £120 a bottle.

Despite his fatigue, he never let autograph hunters down. He signed on book matches, theatre programmes and wine lists for the glowing young girls.

'Oh, Mr Harris,' they'd gush, 'you've got such beautiful legs.' The actor would wince. Each time he was approached with reverence, almost on tiptoe, he removed the preposterous hat in deference to the female sex.

Whenever he had a mishap on tour, the press tended to call it 'the curse of *Camelot*'. Once, he was rushed to the Henry Ford Hospital in Detroit after he complained of a mystery illness. Severe chest pains had forced him to cut short his performance. It was the second time the jinx had struck him. In May he escaped death by a second when he jumped clear as a one-ton set was lowered into position where he stood.

On another occasion, he had to bow out of the show when he developed a spinal infection after an accident in a stage fight. In Detroit, Harris knew it wasn't by any means a serious heart attack, rather total exhaustion from the gruelling tour. In the hospital ward he was in a lively mood and assured everyone he had no intention of dying. It was during an intermission after two hours of a performance at the city's Masonic Auditorium that he told fellow actors, 'I am ill.'

On release from hospital, he had regained some of his old strength, and announced, '*Camelot* has given me a new lease of life.'

During the tour, his wife Ann spent a few days with him. He found it fun, but insisted that he was a man who wanted to be alone and independent, and for a lot of the time completely free. The year before, their marriage had gone through an extremely rocky period and future auguries did not appear too good. With typical arrogance, he had already begun to dictate his own conditions for the survival of the marriage. Ostensibly, it was a selfish act on his part.

'In future I will do as I wish, go off with women when I like, and Annie is completely free to do what ever she wants,' he declared.

At that time Rex Harrison was touring America with *My Fair Lady*, and had married again since the break-up of his marriage to Elizabeth. Harris was soon to break Harrison's box-office record in Los Angeles by doing half a million dollars' worth of business in one week with *Camelot*. 'So I sent Rex a telegram,' he recalled, ' "If you can take my ex-wife I can take your record." I thought it was terribly funny but I didn't get a reply. Elizabeth told me that Rex wouldn't have laughed because he didn't have a sense of humour.'

His success in America that year was tinged with some bitterness. His marriage to Ann Turkel ended in divorce after seven years. A combination of reasons was put forward for the breakdown, among them growing tension between them, and incompatibility. Harris said, 'We're obsessed with each other; it was so intense that it was to the exclusion of everything else and just sort of let our careers slide away.'

Ann was by now thirty-four and more striking than beautiful – a woman who admitted she was still insecure about her looks, who said she had never thought of herself as attractive and never had any social life until she was eighteen. Richard, she said, released everything in her.

'We still love each other,' she continued to assure her rather sceptical friends. 'We'll always love each other. He will never find anyone else who loves him as much as I do.'

There was no reason to doubt her words. She had undeniably put a substantial emotional input into her marriage and it was clear it would take a considerable time for her to get over the trauma of divorce. She reasoned with herself that she had by now matured and would be able to live without Richard, something she was unable to do during most of the seven years of their marriage.

Though she was still close to Harris's three sons and invited them to visit her in Los Angeles, she was assailed by the thought that perhaps she had put too much into her marriage and considered it had been a mistake because her career suffered. For some years she had just been Mrs Richard Harris and not Ann Turkel, actress. In retrospect, she knew this was wrong. She needed to work again, so as to allow herself time to readjust her life and career. She had already succeeded in getting a part in *Modesty Blaise*.

It was clear, though, that she had been hurt more than she liked to admit by her unpredictable husband. She used to tell the world that she had tamed Richard, but she really had to admit to herself that this was not true. The fact was, he was untamable. It was his fear of heart attacks and death that had changed him, not any action on her part, though she had tried pretty hard to alter his image. Harris, despite his generosity of spirit, his gentleness on occasion, could be cruel to the women he loved.

Elizabeth who had been his wife for twelve years, was the first to discover that disturbing reality. In a different way, the experience was to be repeated in her marriage with Rex Harrison: 'After many reconciliations I finally left Rex. I felt very low. I still loved him and he loved me, but we were simply destroying each other.' Meanwhile she continued to follow Richard's career as though she were married again to him.

The trouble with Harris was that he made everything sound rational, even his definition of his 'ideal' relationship with Ann Turkel. As he said, 'My ideal existence would be to have an apartment in New York, my house on Paradise Island and still be able to visit Annie in Los Angeles when I felt like it. Annie and I could have some fun and might go to bed and then I would leave after a little while.'

He had conveniently forgotten that Ann had matured, grown up as a woman, and wanted to pursue her own career. But by now he had become obsessed with *Camelot* and the magnificent new lease of life it had given him. He was already thinking of introducing King Arthur to West End audiences.

Eighteen months after he had made his notable comeback in Los Angeles, he was ensconced in a settee in his luxury London hotel suite and doing the thing he loved best – proclaiming to the world in an Irish brogue his philosophy of life, and his hopes for *Camelot* which was due to open at the Apollo Victoria on 12 November 1982.

Dressed in a Victorian nightshirt, he was stretched on the settee, his head upright, looking more relaxed than pugnacious. As ever, the conversation was peppered with expletives, though the garb looked more *monkish* than shocking.

His press quotes were once again diligently worked on. His best lines were:

> My burning desire is to be a monk ... Women prefer women's company ... I've had enough women in my life to know that lurking under that Helena Rubinstein exterior is a very vicious animal (expletive) insensitive savages, absolutely ruthless ... I've tired of being loved by women. It's the most dangerous trap you can get into. I'd prefer to be cared for ... loving is deceptive passion ... I've done some horrible things to people – things that make me cringe. I've humiliated people – lost my temper – I've hurt people – actors, directors, all sorts of people.

No one could accuse him of being less than frank and honest. A few of his old Fleet Street cronies still could not accept that he was virtually teetotal, so they tended to concentrate their efforts on his conversion. He talked about hypoglycaemia, as if to convince all and sundry that it was the only reason why he was off the booze.

As opening night approached, he was nervous. It seemed years since he was on a London stage. Could he repeat the American success of *Camelot* before West End audiences? Predictably, Harris could be counted upon to add something extra to the occasion. Word had gone out that his ex-wife Ann Turkel was in town and actually sharing his hotel suite. The publicity people were delighted. That unexpected touch of romance ensured that the full glare of publicity was focused on the pair. When Miss Turkel announced that they could end up getting married again, the story looked as though it had been scripted weeks before. 'We probably have the most perfect relationship in the world,' she added gleefully, 'Richard is a genius.'

No one seemed to care that it was an unpleasant, rainy night for the opening. A galaxy of stars could be picked out among the audience, among them Roger Moore and his wife Luisa; Petula Clarke, from a 13-month run in *The Sound of Music*, and Louis

Jourdan with actress Hannah Gordon. The cameras flashed in the foyer as Elizabeth, Harris's ex-wife arrived with her new husband, Peter Aitken, Lord Beaverbrook's grandson.

'We had to come – Richard introduced us!' remarked Aitken. The couple had sent him a plant and a bud for good luck.

From his home town Limerick, a number of relatives and old friends made the journey. 'Dickie invited us,' said one. 'We have been at most of his first nights.'

There was no doubt that Harris was overjoyed at being reunited with his ex-wife Ann. Backstage, she fussed over him. They looked as if they had never been parted. At every opportunity she hugged and kissed 'her king' as she called him. He once said about their divorce, 'It should have been a great two-hour dramatic movie – but it turned into a 32-episode soap opera.'

While the applause of an audience may not always be a true yardstick by which to measure the merit of a play or a musical, the packed audience at the Apollo Victoria gave the production a rousing reception, with Harris's King Arthur being picked out for acclamation. As always, he perspired freely afterwards in his dressing-room and could not possibly greet all the well-wishers who crowded round to shake his hand. But Ann Turkel was there to manage the exciting proceedings, ensuring that Richard wasn't entirely overwhelmed.

The reviews weren't as universally ecstatic in tone as had been the case in America. '*Camelot* is still a special treat for anyone who likes hearing jaunty tunes while looking at Selfridges Christmas windows,' commented *Daily Express* critic David Roper. And he added:

Richard Harris must be nearly 900 years old now. Or is that King Arthur? No, it must be Richard Harris because this is the fourth time he's come back to life in *Camelot*, and he does rather sail through his kingdom with that certain boredom one would have if one had been there that long. But there he is, still in love with Guinevere, still knighting people as if it was the Birthday Honours every day of the year. Only now his hair has faded like parchment. And he doesn't really bother to sing all that much, preferring now to talk his way through songs like Rex Harrison. Poor old King Arthur. He looks so underweight and over-age that you really do believe he was that weedy nit who pulled the sword Excalibur out of the stone by accident. The only thing that keeps him going must be the beautiful Fiona Fullerton who has breathed gold-tressed life into the part of Queen Guinevere.

The *Evening Standard* critic, Milton Shulman told his readers:

Back in 1964 I assessed the musical *Camelot*, as wholesome, pretty and empty. Seeing it again at the Apollo Victoria I felt I had been caught in a time warp. It is still wholesome, pretty and empty. Reviving it after so many years, it is clearly the producer's hope that chivalry is not dead and will prove to be alive and well and thriving at a West End box office.

Being somewhat allergic to the Arthurian legend and its emphasis on virtue as a way of life, I had almost as severe a problem wrestling with sleep as Richard Harris, as Arthur, had wrestling with his conscience.

Richard Harris interprets King Arthur with such restraint that one feels his frequent calls for advice to an unseen Merlin and his agonising over his intellectual capacity indicate an inferiority complex that might have helped had he used his round table as psychiatrist's couch.

Fiona Fullerton, as Guinevere, has just the kind of glacial beauty to justify knights going berserk trying to find monsters to slay on her behalf.

Michael Rudman's direction tried to lift the musical's naïve intellectual content by dampening down the humour and maintaining a note of earnest endeavour. It fully justifies Noel Coward's comment when he first saw it, '*Parsifal* without the jokes.'

Two questions were by now uppermost in the minds of the show-biz fraternity; one, could *Camelot* survive?; two, would Richard Harris remarry Ann Turkel?

It was soon obvious that *Camelot* was in trouble. After the mixed reception by the critics, theatregoers began to stay away. The death knell of the musical was already being sounded. Because he believed totally in the show, Harris made desperate efforts to save it.

He had discussions with his director Michael Rudman and demanded a revamp and drastic cuts. 'I want to go in with major surgery,' he said, brushing aside Rudman's protests. It was the old, fiery, autocratic Harris storming the scene, refusing to listen to advice.

It was no surprise when Rudman resigned after what was described as a series of backstage jousts. It was a gentle way of putting it. Harris could be heard shouting at the director on more than one occasion. 'Either you do what I say, or you go.'

A statement was put out that 'Rudman resigned over a difference of artistic opinion.'

Nearer the point was that the director would not agree to wholesale changes. An Apollo spokesman said, 'It is agreed that Mr Rudman's departure is in the show's best interests.'

Frank Dunlop, who directed Harris on tour in America, flew from New York to take over direction.

Harris tried to explain away the failure of the show at the box-office by claiming that he had wanted to delay the opening night by two weeks because he did not feel the production was as good as it could be but the producer's hand resisted his move.

He said he had also wanted to cut fifteen to twenty minutes in the first act because he felt it was too long. Rudman refused. Harris thought the director's attitude was 'unforgivable'. It struck him that he had resisted restaging someone else's work but had failed to replace it with something that was exciting. Coming close to the opening he thought it was far too long and a lot of Frank Dunlop's invention was missing.

'I have a reputation for being difficult to work with,' he added, 'but that's because I am a perfectionist. But this time I thought I would turn over a new leaf and sit very quietly and let it take its course. I should have stayed the Richard Harris of old and insisted that either he went or I went.' He conceded that Michael Rudman had a high reputation as a director but he felt he had approached *Camelot* as if it was a serious, earthbound production. 'We need to put the wings back on it.'

Rehearsals proceeded under Frank Dunlop's direction. Harris, who had been in danger of collapsing during the controversy, relaxed and everyone hoped for a 'cure'. A rescue plan was worked out. But soon the plan to transfer the show to the Phoenix Theatre was scrapped. 'It is not economically viable,' a spokesman announced.

Harris's pride was hurt. He could not understand why West-Enders had rejected the musical after its success in America. He agreed to relinquish his fixed salary. By late January 1983, it was decided, however, to end the show's run. Harris was bitterly disappointed; more than anything else he wanted to come back in triumph to the West End with the musical.

Camelot general manager Peter Schneider admitted that business in the West End was bad. 'I think Richard is very disappointed – I think we are all disappointed.'

It did not help the star's ego that Ann Turkel had returned to Los Angeles, telling the world that she had no plans to remarry Richard Harris.

For the time being, King Arthur had not only lost his throne but also the woman he hoped to remarry. The fates were again unkind to him as he prepared to journey back to his Paradise Island. He could be excused for humming an appropriate number from *Camelot*, 'I Loved You Once in Silence'.

Already, however, he had plans to buy the rights of *Camelot* and to bring it on tour throughout America. Failure in the West End did not, in his eyes, mean the end of his love affair with *Camelot*.

20   *Death of a brother*

There are only two ways to reach his Paradise retreat – boat and breaststroke. One day, the story goes, Michael Caine came to visit him. He took a look around and said, 'I wouldn't mind buying a place down here.'

Harris looked at him in mock dismay, 'Please don't! I came this far to get away from it all – don't bring it with you!'

He had a recurring nightmare, it was said, of waking up one sunny morning and finding his old hellraising buddy, Malachy McCourt had bought the island over his head.

Whatever else he may have lost, including two wives, Harris retained his puckish humour and sense of mischief. Even the nightmarish thought of McCourt landing on Paradise Island, sporting a beard, made him laugh in a wicked way. It was his love of humour and mischief, friends claimed, that helped him to survive the traumas of two broken marriages.

When he was expecting people to call on him at his island home, he usually set off to greet them in a motor launch. One visitor who was met in this way, writer Leila Farrah, once described him as 'a fugitive from the pages of Graham Greene'. It was Harris's unkempt appearance that captivated her; he happened to be wearing a loose white vest carelessly tucked into white trousers.

Undeniably, he was able to get away from it all here. When neighbours on Paradise Island took to dropping by uninvited, he conceived an impish plot to deter them. One afternoon, a family living close by turned up with their house guests to pay a social call. They found the star with his brother Dermot and a male friend watching a blue movie. The three of them were naked. 'Oh, hello there.' Harris called out amiably. 'Come on in.' The visitors fled.

'Did you see their faces?' he said, roaring with laughter. It was the old prankster in Harris let loose again. He loved nothing better than pulling an outrageous trick on people. He kept the film in case anyone else called. No one ever did.

He was close to his brother Dermot, who was by now his business manager and ran a lucrative music company in London. Together, in previous years, they used to rent a house in Stroud in the Cotswolds and were joined there by their wives and families. 'We had a wonderful time,' recalls Harris.

When he bought the rights of *Camelot* and decided to launch himself on another tour with the show, he appointed Dermot as producer. 'I own *Camelot* lock stock and barrel,' he liked to say. 'It's a huge moneymaker.'

It was true. Since he started touring the show he grossed millions of dollars. He had plans to bring it to Japan and Canada. The American public showed an insatiable interest in the musical, and Harris played to packed houses. 'It was astonishing,' he says, 'the way they received us. England could never muster up their kind of enthusiasm for King Arthur and his royal court.'

Tragedy, however, struck in Chicago in 1986. Dermot was busy producing the show and was having a hectic time. One evening, he said to Richard, 'Dick, I don't feel too good. I'll go and lie down.'

'Look after yourself,' Harris told his younger brother. Later, he went on stage wearing his crown and cloak but when he came off again Dermot was dead.

'That's when everything fell into place,' recalls Harris sadly today. 'Dermot was such a rogue. You can take me and magnify me ten times, that was my brother. He'd say to me, "You go and do that picture so I can live in the style to which I've become accustomed."

'The great mystery was solved when I saw him on a slab in the hospital, his face purple from a massive heart attack. And that's what it's all about, isn't it? Here and gone. Why do we mess it up? We want too much and we're not pleased with what we have.'

For years Dermot would videotape all international rugby matches involving Ireland and send them on to Paradise Island. On Saturday afternoons Harris would play them back on his video machine, and his bellowing and blaspheming at the Irish pack could sometimes be heard by the crews of the passing yachts.

Dermot's remains were flown to Limerick for burial. Harris

attended the funeral and immediately afterwards flew by Concord to Baltimore, Maryland to resume his stage role of King Arthur. Those close to him felt he was shattered by his brother's unexpected death and was anxious that his memory be perpetuated. He quickly set about establishing the Dermot Harris Foundation which would grant one student per year a scholarship to study at the University of Scranton in Pennsylvania.

It illustrated once again the thoughtful side of the star – the side which some of his detractors unfairly ignored. In interviews, he talked about the death of his brother and how it had affected his own life. He told one journalist, 'My brother Dermot died last year of – there is no doubt – excessive drinking. A heart attack. And I walked around saying, "If only I'd known he had the pain in his chest, I could have got him into hospital and he could have had a quadruple by-pass or whatever." All his friends laugh at me! They said, "If you said to Dermot you're going to die at such a date if you don't stop drinking, smoking and sitting around in bars, he'd say, 'Okay, I'll go then.' " He probably had more guts than I. I don't want to go. I'm enjoying my life. But then I really don't need drink any more. I can find the excessiveness in theatre or in cinema or in conversation.'

The death of close friends greatly affected him. He broke down a few years before when he gave a eulogy as Hollywood paid a final tribute to Richard Burton. He had begun his tribute with the lines from Shakespeare's *Richard II*, 'Let us sit upon the ground ...' when he hurried from the stage overcome by emotion. The lines continue '... and tell sad stories of the death of Kings'.

Harris returned shortly afterwards. He told the audience gathered at the Wiltshire Theater, 'If Richard had seen me a moment ago he would have been howling with laughter.'

The late 1980s had not been the best period for him – with the divorce from his second wife Ann Turkel, his son Jamie's problem with heroin, and the tragedy of his beloved brother Dermot's death at the age of forty-eight. But he managed to soften the blows by standing by his son; he understood the problem perhaps better than most fathers since, on his own admission, he took drugs himself in the mid-1970s.

'Yes, for nine months I used to really swallow cocaine. I didn't know it was dangerous. Then I ended up in the Cedars of Lebanon. Later, I went home and threw about 6,000 dollars' worth down the toilet and I haven't touched it since.'

Jamie Harris's plight was not only a serious worry to Richard but to Elizabeth, his mother. Like her ex-husband, she was able to say, 'I am fully behind Jamie.'

Undoubtedly, their son's problem had brought the Harrises closer together. Elizabeth changed her name back to Harris. By the mid-1980s her marriage to Peter Aitken was over after only four years. She was living permanently in London again and had moved into a £400,000 house. She claimed that she received nothing but maintenance from Harris but that Rex Harrison was 'very generous' on their divorce.

At the same time, Harris was declaring his love for Elizabeth and, in a typical grand gesture, splashed out £16,000 to buy her a new car for her birthday. 'I still love her,' he proclaimed.

He described her as 'an incredible woman' and vowed he would do anything for her, except remarry her. His reason, which seemed acceptable to most people was, that he was 'impossible to live with'. He said he loved giving her surprises. His good humour surfaced when he said, 'I used to get engaged at least three times a week and would even fall in love with the barman if he gave me a double brandy. I gave Liz hell and I'm glad she gave me the boot. I deserved it. But I'd do anything for Liz and my family.'

Damian was by now 27, Gerard 25, and Jamie 23. Funnily, Elizabeth, who knew that her ex-husband possessed a wicked sense of humour, first thought that he was only joking about the new car for her birthday present. It was a wonderful surprise, she said.

Elizabeth was now able to reflect on their broken marriage and pinpoint where things went wrong. 'I did a lot of things that I now wish I hadn't done. The slanging matches and the punch-ups have all been reported. But there were times when we would fall about with laughter.'

But she wondered now if they had been wrong to pack their sons off to boarding school while they jetted between film locations. When son Jamie came to her house a few years before, desperate and penniless through his dependence on drugs, she nursed him through his terrible hallucinations and convulsions.

She said that Richard had been incredibly supportive to her. 'We have spent lots of holidays together. We spent last Christmas together on Paradise Island with all the family. He has been wonderful with the boys; he's involved with all of them and their lives.'

In the early days of marriage they must have been the only theatrical couple who talked rugby together. Elizabeth says she had been brought up in a rugby family. 'At every Sunday lunch my family relived Saturday's match.' She had been asked more than once what she thought of today's Richard Harris. Usually she reflected for a moment before answering, as though she still wasn't sure about his make-up.

'You may think him an extrovert,' she said, 'but he's not really. He has always entered into the spirit of things in a very rumbustious way. He liked to get the best out of a situation. When he meets people he gives them great attention; he is extraordinarily interested in people. But, as at the same time he is a very private person I would describe him as an incredibly private extrovert.'

She reckoned that giving up the drink had made him more objective. He read voraciously and was very well informed. He had a very panoramic view of life, but he could still blow a gasket. She saw him turning to writing in his later years.

Today, Ann Turkel lives in Beverly Hills and says she had no regrets about her marriage to Harris. 'I learned so much from Richard it was like being born again. We were seven years together, after all.' She admits that when she first met him, he was still gallivanting, but during their married years he tended to live a pretty reclusive life. 'We went to the odd screening or the odd première, but if we went out five times a year that was the most.'

She was proud of his record. As she emphasized, 'I can't think of any other actor who has starred in movies, starred on Broadway in musicals, won awards, collected Emmys and Gold Discs, published poetry, written songs, produced and directed plays and movies, recorded songs. He has had careers in almost every field of activity in the arts – except painting. I remember when we went to Richard Burton's memorial service in Hollywood, people were saying how versatile he had been. But really, nobody has done as much as Richard, and he hasn't been given the credit. Others with a tenth of his talent have been hailed for doing little. And when they are asked for an autograph I've seen them push the fans away. Yet I've seen Richard after a matinee of *Camelot* dropping with exhaustion, yet obliging people at the stage door who wanted his autograph or a picture.'

Like Elizabeth Harris, Ann praised his generosity. He gave himself to so many people on so many levels. She said she had noted changes in her former husband's attitude after David Janssen died. David and his wife Danny were close friends of theirs. On the day he died – it was Valentine's Day – she remembered they were in New York. When they got the call that he had passed away, Richard was so terribly upset he left the apartment and disappeared for five hours. She didn't know where he had gone. Afterwards she discovered he had been sitting on the steps of St Patrick's. The cathedral was closed, so he sat outside for hours in the middle of winter. The second time was when Richard Burton died. And then his brother Dermot. Richard's religion did not have any bearing on her own day-to-day life, nor his, but maybe he had got closer to God.

Their marriage over, Ann was said to have offered to adopt her former husband. 'Although I go out with a guy now, I still feel close to Richard. When we divorced, our relationship never changed. We are still just as close as when we were married. If anything happened to Richard I would be destroyed.'

Despite his leisurely time in the Bahamas, Harris was still in the market for work. His tour of *Camelot* over, he accepted an offer to portray the detective Maigret in a new television movie.

He first read a Maigret story in 1972 when he was introduced to Simenon's detective by John Huston. He said he was instantly hooked and went on to read sixty or seventy of them. It had been an obsession of his to play Maigret ever since. George Weingarten, an American producer and writer, spent thirteen years getting the world rights to Maigret stories and then getting them to the screen. Before Weingarten's acquisition, the rights to individual Maigret stories had been sold to countries all over the world so that there were dozens of Maigret's of different nationalities – there had even been a Japanese Maigret. That would all stop now.

'The clue to Maigret,' said Harris, 'is that he watches

everything and throws people into psychological con-
frontations.'

Weingarten was introduced to 85-year-old Georges Simenon,
the author of the Maigret books, by a mutual friend, Graham
Greene. Simenon did not ask who would play the part in the
television series. When he was told Richard Harris, he said, 'I
would never have thought of him in a million years. My
favourite was Jean Gabin in France who made seven films, but
now you say it, I can see him.' The only other question he asked
was how Harris would look. When he heard about the old
clothes which seemed to have come from Oxfam, the duffle coat
and hat without a stiffener inside, Simenon was happy.

To make himself appear more plodding, Harris wore size 15
shoes (instead of his normal 9½), and his naturally tall and lean
frame looked bulky in his Maigret outfit – which took him all of
ten minutes to choose. It was five years since he had made a
movie. He had no qualms, he said, about playing Maigret. The
original British Maigret, Rupert Davies, who played the
detective on BBC TV from 1960 to 1964 (he died in 1976), became
so involved in the part that he could play no other.

The new Maigret had been brought into the Eighties, though
he remained essentially a man of the Fifties. He didn't much
care for the telephone and would have nothing to do with police
computers. Harris planned to use a slight Scots accent with the
emphasis on the 'r's and brought his voice almost to a croak.

Maigret was filmed in colour on location in Paris. It would be
screened as a two-hour television Movie of the Week and, if that
was considered successful, just two films of other Simenon stories
every eighteen months. There would be no weekly drudge, no
dangers of over-identification for cast or crew. As in the original
BBC series the new Maigret would be shown together with his
wife. In all the 104 Simenon books about the detective, his wife
was seldom mentioned and only once by her name, Louise.

'He never referred to her by her first name,' said Harris, who
had read most of the books. 'It is always Madame and he was
Monsieur, and in all the years they have been married, he never
observes the changes in her or in their relationship. So as he
tries to solve the murder of an old friend, he is also seeking clues
to what happened to their marriage. It has soured – like a love
affair that has gone to sleep.' Harris's wife in the series was
played by Barbara Shelley.

Harris approached the television movie with his usual enthusiasm and zest. Strangely, it did not make an impact when screened. The critics panned it; an older generation of British viewers were unable to erase the memory of Rupert Davies from their minds, and the general consensus of opinion was that Harris did not make a truly convincing detective. Taking the stories out of their time did not work; in the minds of most people it remained a Fifties series.

Harris was philosophical. 'I gave it all I got,' he mused. 'It's still a bloody good movie.'

Despite the luxury of his surroundings in the Bahamas, he tended in the late 1980s to return to Ireland more frequently, though on his own admission he found the country 'very difficult'. As he explained, 'Going to Ireland and not going to a bar is like going to church and not saying a prayer. To go to Ireland and have all your mates say to you, "Go on, Dick, have a drink!" The Irish philosophy is that they'd rather die than give it up. "What kind of pussycat are you?" they ask. "Die laughing! Don't be bored to death! Drink and die!" '

But he stands firm, despite his fond nostalgia for 'the hard stuff'. Although he makes no secret of his dislike of interviews, in May 1988 he did talk candidly to writer Joe Jackson from Ireland's most influential pop magazine *Hot Press*. Regrettably, many of his friends missed the interview because the magazine normally only appealed to the under-30s age group.

It was a kind of brief run-through of his life – and career – with no punches pulled, as can be seen from some of the questions and answers:

Many would class as a downward move the journey from This Sporting Life *to being Bo Derek's father in* Tarzan.
I have no regrets. I loved every minute of that movie. I love Bo Derek and I was a great friend of John Derek so I had a fantastic time doing that picture.

At the beginning of your career you seemed to be trying to operate two careers in tandem, the Antonioni-type art-film balanced against commercial fodder. Of late however, the films seem to lean in the latter direction.
(*Laughs*) In the beginning I did try to do interesting films. But

there comes a time when you are faced with obligations.
You've got a wife to support, and children, and you want
them to have what you didn't have. You can't support that on
art-films. I remember the day I made the choice. I'm not
making excuses. These were the realities. I had children and
we were living in a tiny flat in London sleeping together, all of
us, in two rooms. And though there was no pressure from
Elizabeth I sat down and said, I've got a choice here. I can do
The Luck of Ginger Coffee – it's a fantastic piece but it will pay
only what I got for *This Sporting Life* – or I can get a fortune to
do *Major Dundee* in Hollywood. And the latter is the choice I
made. The choice was the right choice, I still believe.

*So you wouldn't agree with the movie dictionary review of your
career which says 'failed to live up to the promise he showed as an
actor'?*
What promise? His? The guy who wrote the dictionary? Why
should I feel obliged to live up to his expectations? Who is he
to pass judgement? If I had my life to live over I'd do the same
things again. The only difference, in terms of my career, is
that I wouldn't stay away from stage for so long. '64–'81 was a
mistake. But I've acknowledged it, there's nothing I can do
about that. I can't regret it. I've done more than most.

Why have you decided to go back to making movies?
Because I'm going to do *my own* pictures. I don't want to get
involved in what I call the Hollywood Picture – big budget
pictures where everybody is telling you what to do because it
costs 15 million. If you make a 3–5 million dollar movie, no
one interferes, so you can make it, be proud of it, then move
on. I want to get involved in *This Sporting Life* type pictures
again. Small, intimate and with substance. I've read two
things I love. And I'm glad I stayed away for long enough to
rethink the rest of my life. I think I've revitalized myself. I feel
that, like Lazarus, I've come back from the dead!

In all areas of your life?
Well, I had a very bad second marriage too. Not through any
fault of Ann's. It was a bad time in my life. It was like Burton
and Taylor, an all-consuming relationship. Look at me now,
full of energy, right? If Ann Turkel called now and I spoke to
her for ten minutes, I'd have to say 'the interview is over, Joe,

call you Tuesday'. She'd drain everything out of me. She fed on it. She couldn't help it. It was something you couldn't extradite yourself from, it was just there. You'd try to solve it, get out – you couldn't.

The darkness in a relationship like that can be attractive to some people.
There had to be some kind of attraction in all that, yes, otherwise I wouldn't have stuck with it so long.

Do you think we learn from the failure of a first marriage – or do we make the same mistakes all over again?
This is interesting. I broke up my first marriage because I was totally selfish, right? The second one broke up because I was selfless. I did everything. I was like a nursemaid. I was a father, uncle, lover, doctor, psychiatrist, occasional husband, father-confessor in her eyes. It broke up because I couldn't take that any more. I gave too much because the first one was an absolute catastrophic fuck-up because of my behaviour – and so I tried to over-compensate in the second.

Atoning for your sins, reacting to the then rather than the now?
Exactly, and that was disastrous.

Is that what has left you so bitter about marriage?
I'm not bitter.

'Marriage is a custom thought up by women where they proceed to live off men ... eating them away like poison fungus on a tree.'
(*Laughs*) Did I say that? That's lovely, isn't it?

But is it how you feel?
I don't feel bitter or angry. That there is a perfect description by a man who's been through it all, who says 'This is what it is.' Coolly, calmly, simply.

Did you ever regard any woman as your equal?
I got carried away there (*laughs*). If I worked with Vanessa Redgrave again I'd consider us as equals, absolutely. She is a tremendous woman. And Joan Littlewood, who started me out in theatre. She was superior and would be today. So women like that, people like that, yes.

So you accept that there are women and men on different levels and in different capacities, who are your superiors?

My God you have to. How else could we learn? I'm a better actor than a lot of people and many – well, a few – are better than me (*laughs*). But as a human being how am I to know – or rather who am I to say?

Do you suffer from that 'star disease' of thinking that because fans continually tell you so, you must really be 'a wonderful person'?
No. (*Laughs*) I know I'm not wonderful. Not at all.

A bit of a shithead at times?
Of course I am but then aren't we all at times. But I do accept that there is a dark and potentially unpleasant and potentially violent side to my nature. Whether other people can accept that about me or about themselves, really is their problem.

Drinking has drastically altered your life. The special diet you're on, the fact that you can't drink ...
Well, I have a choice now. My choice is 'If you take a drink tonight you could go into a coma and be dead tomorrow.'

What, finally, made you stop?
When someone did say, to me 'You'll be dead within six months if you don't.' I stopped overnight. Same with regards to the four packs of cigarettes I used to smoke a day. I stopped overnight simply because I found myself out of breath on stage.

Didn't the spur to stop drinking also come from some form of mental split during 'Cromwell' – that you were so overtaken by the part that you started roaring down the phone 'We must give Charles the First another chance'?
But I didn't finally stop till 1981 ... That was 1970 and I went off drinking then, yet I started about a year later because I felt I was in control again. I felt I was the jockey on the wild horse and I could either let it go or pull back.

But during 'Cromwell' you lost control?
And that was a terrifying experience. I actually woke up that morning and thought we were cutting the head off Charles the First.

Yet you still find it difficult to suggest that such substances as drink and drugs are safer taken in moderation?
I think the more pressure you put on people the more you

can aggravate a situation. If someone genuinely said to me tomorrow, 'I want to stop drinking,' I'd say 'I did it – here's how.' If they said 'I want to stop taking drugs,' I'd help them. But when we move into the private sector and say, 'You can't do this, you can't do that', then it gets dangerous. I'm against governments in the private sector. Their job is to balance the economy, give people work, look after private property – but it really is none of their business to tell me that, in America for instance, I can't have a drink before 5 p.m. if I want one. Or to tell me I can't take drugs. It's none of their business to tell me what I can and can't do with my life.

21   *A man called 'Bull'*

He was relaxing in his island hacienda when he was offered a starring role in a movie called *The Field*, which would be shot in Ireland that autumn of 1989. Originally the part of Bull McCabe had been allotted to Ray McAnally, but when he died suddenly at his home in County Wicklow the producer of the new movie, Noel Pearson decided that Harris was the best possible replacement.

The star jumped at the opportunity to play Bull McCabe, even though it would be twenty-five years since he worked for so small a pay packet. When he studied the script by Jim Sheridan, who had directed the much acclaimed *My Left Foot*, the story of the paraplegic Christy Brown, he described it as 'mighty'.

'I've waited my entire career for something as good as this,' Harris enthused. 'As I told my Hollywood agent, William Shakespeare wrote two plays to really test actors – *Hamlet*, to stretch the young actor to the limits, and *King Lear*, for the older actor who could make that leap. For me, *This Sporting Life* was my *Hamlet* and *The Field* will be my *Lear*.'

McAnally had portrayed the awesome Bull McCabe on the stage in Dublin and was keen to make him a screen hero. 'The role is made for the big screen,' McAnally told producer Noel Pearson at the time. 'I want to play it.' Bull McCabe is the central character in playwright John B. Keane's drama, *The Field*, the tale of murder and revenge over the acquisition of land in County Kerry. Jim Sheridan, who adapted the play for the screen, decided to shoot the movie in County Galway.

Accompanied by his son Jamie, who would be the runner on the film set, Harris left his island retreat in October and set out for Ireland. Thirty years before, he had had a small part in *Shake Hands with the Devil* made at Ardmore Studios in Bray. His enthusiasm for *The Field* soon turned into an obsession; director Jim Sheridan, who sweated over the script, was in the same frame of mind.

It was only his second movie, and he was anxious to follow

My Left Foot with another artistic and commercial success. For
Harris, now more mellowed, *The Field* was considered crucial to
the future of his acting career. In the 1980s, he had virtually
turned his back on movie-making and retreated with
uncharacteristic calm to the seclusion of his home on Paradise
Island. There was a decided hint of bitterness as he explained, 'I
turned down most of the offers because there are too many
artless savages out there who simply want to rent your face and
then ruin what you do.'

It was part of the truth. Another reason was that lack of
personal satisfaction with the roles he had played in a succession
of routine and worthless movies had sapped his energy and
enthusiasm. In conversation, he was frank about the disasters: 'I
went through a time when I didn't care what films I did – I just
hired them my body and my voice. Work had taken a secondary
place in my life. I picked easy scripts that I could walk through,
and not have to deliver or really perform. It was easy money.'

Money, like property, had always attracted him. He could be
careful, even tight, with money, and money often figured in
interviews he gave the press. He tried to explain away his film
disasters by saying that he wanted to make sure that he had
enough money to take care of his three sons and ex-wife
Elizabeth. He confided to a Limerick friend that the divorce
settlement in the case of his second wife, Ann Turkel, had cost
him 'two million dollars'. But in the same voice he would later
enthuse over the millions he had made out of *Camelot*. He liked
to boast of his earnings and he had a ready audience.

Nonetheless, poor movies had damaged his reputation as an
actor and, in the film world, lost him some degree of respect. His
shameful neglect of the stage was inexplicable and deliberate.
Such was his total commitment to movies that he scarcely bothered considering offers to play stage roles, even *Hamlet* which he
always said he wanted to do. Yet, he rarely mentioned the film
flops, preferring to recall *This Sporting Life*, *Cromwell*, *Major
Dundee*, *The Heroes of Telemark*, *Camelot* and one or two others.
When producer Noel Pearson came along with the offer of *The
Field* Harris quickly recognized the potential in the part of Bull
McCabe and saw the film as a possible means of re-establishing
his waning career. It was a grand new challenge. If other producers and directors had lost faith in him, Pearson certainly had
not. He believed in his acting ability and pulling-power on screen.

It was noticeable at the first Dublin press conference to announce his role in *The Field* that he was determined to give the impression of starting anew. 'I want to make worthwhile movies again,' he said with a grin. It was the old Richard Harris talking, as in the halcyon days of *This Sporting Life*, once more bubbling with zest and enthusiasm. He just could not wait to get to the location set of *The Field*, where, in a tiny village, one of the biggest challenges of his career awaited him.

The village of Leenane, County Galway, is picturesque and overshadowed by the peaks of the Twelve Pins. On the day Harris arrived it was being transformed. Workmen in heavy-duty denims were stapling sheets of roughened paper to the facade of Gaynor's pub, removing the Shell sign from the crossroads and carefully dismantling the thoroughly modern kilometer roadsigns from the stone bridge. An appropriate monument would be fitted over the steel-framed public phone kiosk and a 40ft-high 'castle' would conceal the inappropriate candy-pink private house on the Letterfrack end of the village.

The parish priest, Fr. Paul Costello suggested that the producer Noel Pearson leave his own name and the name of his movie over the door of Gaynor's pub after the completion of the movie. 'It will be a nice tourist attraction,' said the genial priest, who remembered when they filmed *The Quiet Man* 'next door' in County Mayo. Now he stood in his Sunday pulpit and exhorted his parishioners to give Noel Pearson and the entire cast and crew of Ferndale Films every help they could. It was, after all, in the interests of Leenane and the three hundred people who lived within the four-mile radius. Fr. Costello gave the lead. He handed over the parochial hall to the wardrobe department and 'We're doing up the graveyard for them,' he intoned.

Leenane lies at the heart of the most doleful valley of mists and rainbows. The making there of the $7 million movie would bring new prosperity. For the two months of shooting, the little community would be boosted by one hundred crew and cast. Harris grew a beard for the part of Bull McCabe. He now looked more like a native philosopher fisherman than a movie star. He stayed in Renvyle House Hotel, and the chef cooked him special sugar-free dishes.

Staying with him was suntanned, pony-tailed Jamie Harris who was starting his film career at the bottom. Harris himself looked dramatically languid in black cord jeans, a purple Vnecked sweater, and a green scarf knotted at his throat. He swore to all and sundry that he had butterflies. The film was important to him. It was his big comeback.

Every afternoon he went into Gaynor's pub and sat teetotal with the locals to acquaint himself better with his character, Bull McCabe. Every evening he went to his hotel room and memorized his lines, reciting them in monotone for recording on cassette tape. For breakfast, he ate two bowls of oatmeal and bananas and such simple dishes as corned beef, bacon and cabbage and Irish stew for dinner.

'He's a diabetic so we have to be careful about what he eats,' confided a young waitress. 'But he's no trouble at all. He goes round hugging all the girls.'

While Harris moved easily round Renvyle House, the most westerly hotel in Europe, his co-stars were nowhere to be seen. Tom Berenger had just flown in from New York and was resting in his room after leaving strict instructions that he was not to be disturbed. John Hurt, whose film credits included *The Elephant Man* and *Midnight Express*, had moved out of the hotel and into one of the four beach lodges.

Like the village of Leenane itself, *The Field* was expected to be tough, brutal and painful. The Connemara village was chosen as the location because it was manageable in photographic terms, and sufficiently dismal in its geography.

Harris had talked a lot to director Jim Sheridan about the script, and came up with shifts in emphasis and some new ideas. He loved the way Sheridan, who is small in physique, was obsessed with the film they were both going to make. Sheridan, at first, said *Macbeth*, but Harris was sure that *King Lear* was the play they should be thinking of. He was not prepared to play the role of Bull McCabe as though he were a small man who loses his temper over a field and thus came to grief. He said he wanted to play The Bull as a tragic hero, a man with a passionate nobility and pride, who had been slighted. A man whose tragic flaw was his tragic gift as well, whose fate was beyond his own design.

As the days wore on, Harris became a kind of father figure for the crew, cast and locals. For his fifty-eighth birthday, the local people baked a large cake and he was photographed with a group of children. The star was surprised. 'I'm lost for words,' he said. He was invited to open Connemara Sea Week in Letterfrack and in his speech called for the preservation of the beautiful region.

He became the darling of the local children in Leenane, and was genuinely liked. Since half the population was under the age of twenty they may not have even been aware of his old reputation as a hellraiser. A few old-timers wondered whether this venerable-looking figure in a white beard was really cut out to be the fierce Bull McCabe. But Harris persisted in emphasizing the dignity of the man as opposed to his raw brutality.

To onlookers, the star was full of energy and enthusiasm, yet at pains to project his professionalism. He said he knew he was going to make at least one more good movie. He had thought his career had come to an end not with a bang but with a whimper until he was offered the part of Bull McCabe. Now he brooded over the script and wondered if it was possible to get it right.

He had become interested in Ireland again. A few months before he had seen *A Whistle in the Dark* and was impressed by the direction of the work by Gary Hynes. Curiously, when Irish journalists wrote in depth about his career they tended to be over-critical, sometimes dismissive. One of the newspapers had written a profile of him, and almost every single detail was wrong. The profile suggested that his house in the Bahamas was seedy and dilapidated.

'It is worth six million dollars,' Harris said. He was not prepared to accept insults in his own country. He was proud of the achievements of his two sons who had established themselves in acting and movies. One had just directed *The Rachel Papers*, based on the novel by Martin Amis, which received impressive reviews in New York when it opened. The other son had joined the Royal Shakespeare Company as an actor.

Occasionally he thought of coming back to live in Ireland, perhaps in Dingle, County Kerry. In an interview with Dublin's *Sunday Independent*, he surprised some people by admitting that he was dyslexic. He had always read with great difficulty, although when he went through something for the second time he could remember it forever. But when he read a page for the first time, he had no idea what the print said.

'It colours everything: you learn to listen and observe, you become keen and attentive, you can hear what is going on in the next room. You learn to develop tricks that ordinary humans don't have, your way of gathering information is completely different than that of most mortals. You never read the small print, it has to be explained to you; you take nothing for granted, it makes you a good businessman.'

Over the years he had been questioned a lot about his school days at Crescent College in Limerick and whether the Jesuits had any influence on him. In the middle of making *The Field*, he was surprised to learn that his old Alma Mater had decided to honour him. Since he hadn't always been kind to them in his references, he was grateful now. He had a soft spot for Crescent College because it was there that he first acquired his love of rugby football.

Although he had always loved his home town Limerick, it was strangely only in the past few years that he had started to think about it. As he said, 'I've come to believe that a man doesn't care a damn about his childhood until he reaches my age. Then, for some reason, it becomes more important to you.'

Back in Renvyle House he chatted with his son Jamie; they were close and Harris seemed happy to have him around. Jamie made no secret of his determination to make films his career.

Predictably, Harris himself caused a stir in the fishing village. In a gesture of thanks to the people of Leenane – and to the surprised delight of the parish priest – he arrived in the village for Mass on a Sunday and as soon as the words 'thanks be to God' had been uttered in the church, invited everyone back to the pub for drinks on him. Pints and shorts for the elders; lemonade and crisps for the little ones.

Over their pints of Guinness and shorts, the men agreed that Richard Harris was a true born-again Catholic, and as generous as hell. They toasted the bearded star and wished his Bull McCabe well. With the blessing of the parish priest on his head, Harris endeared himself to the locals who were disappointed they could not return his generosity. It wasn't the same when the 'other fellow wasn't drinking'.

Harris guessed what his countrymen were thinking, but he nodded and smiled and refused to accept their drinks. He was no longer in the game of buying popularity. On his part, it was just a spontaneous gesture with no strings attached.

He was enjoying his homecoming, even if he continued to worry how Bull McCabe should be played. Jim Sheridan was happy that he was getting it right and told Harris to relax. To Sheridan, who had directed Daniel Day-Lewis in *My Left Foot*, Christy Brown posed more screen problems than did Bull McCabe.

Harris had by now become the funny man on location of *The Field*. At breakfast in the dining room of Renvyle House he prowled among the tables of cereals and fruit and juices muttering loudly, 'Oranges and bananas and muesli and all this crap that's supposed to be good for you.' The room dissolved in laughter.

Into all this fitted that most British of British actors, John Hurt, cast as the maliciously sly village informer Bird O'Donnell, and scurrying about in tattered old clothes. Hurt had made the part his own, even down to having a cap extracted in the cause of having a mouthful of yukkie molars. Producer Noel Pearson was calling Harris, Hurt and Tom Berenger his 'three musketeers'.

That morning they had been filming a key episode in *The Field*. The field in the story is being auctioned with Bull McCabe confident of buying it without a rival bid. Berenger, as the wealthy American, comes on the scene, but Harris menacingly approaches him to warn him off. There is a palpable hatred in the air between the two actors as they square up to each other. After the shout of 'cut' Berenger dismisses any notion that the hostility on set spills over into real life. 'Not at all,' he says. 'Richard and I get on very well together. We can switch off the animosity as soon as the camera stops turning.' He is wearing a fedora, and dressed in cashmere greatcoat; they create the Bogart aura.

Berenger agreed with Harris that the Italians and the French would enjoy *The Field* for it deals with the nobility of farmers and the peasantry. Veteran actor John Cowley, who had worked with Harris years before in *Shake Hands with the Devil*, is cast as the village auctioneer. Harris says, 'I remember the movie well. A lot of water has flowed under the bridge since then, and a lot of beer has flowed into my belly.'

Everybody has been asking how producer Pearson had managed to get Harris from the Bahamas and Berenger from Hollywood to this remote part of Ireland. 'Richard Harris simply wanted to do the movie,' says Pearson, 'and getting Tom Berenger was a lucky break. He happened to be touring with his family in Ireland and got in touch with me. I offered him the part of the American and over dinner with Richard Harris and Jim Sheridan he accepted.'

Directors and actors who worked with him tend to remember Harris as though it were only yesterday.

Andrew V. McLaglen was happy to recall their months in South Africa filming *The Wild Geese*. McLaglen has directed thirty-one movies and in the autumn of 1989 was working on

Eye of the Widow, an adventurous story in the James Bond mould, at Twickenham Studios. Location work had taken him to half a dozen places throughout the world. Although he had not met Harris for some years, he remembered vividly his work on *The Wild Geese*. 'Richard is a fine actor and it is a pity that *Camelot* took up so much of his time. He should have been making more good movies instead of touring the musical around America.' Today, the director sometimes runs the video of *The Wild Geese* at his home and is invariably impressed by Harris's performance in the final dramatic scene. 'I guess it was the happiest movie I ever made,' McLaglen reflected during a break in the filming of *Eye of the Widow*.

Dana Wynter was still living in County Wicklow and doing more writing and travelling than acting. Whenever Richard Harris's name came up in conversation she recalled working with him in *Shake Hands with the Devil* and now expressed admiration at his undoubted durability as an actor. She particularly liked his King Arthur in *Camelot*. To Cyril Cusack, Harris was simply 'a star of international status'.

From his home in Los Angeles, director Ken Hughes reflected on Harris, then said, 'I guess it's true what they say about Richard – I mean that he's reformed?' Hughes remembered his *Cromwell*, but found it hard to accept that the actor was fighting a drink problem at the time. All he would say was, 'I know one thing, it didn't affect his performance as Cromwell.'

J.P. Donleavy, the author of *The Ginger Man*, was at this time living in a big house in the Irish countryside and writing books. In the neighbourhood he was called the 'Ginger Man', but since the early Sixties he had lost touch with Harris. He was still convinced, though, that he was the 'perfect Ginger Man'.

Sean Connery, who had made two movies with Harris, *The Molly Maguires* and *Robin and Marian*, was still friendly with Harris and wanted to know when they were going to get together again on a movie. 'Richard and I enjoyed good times filming together,' he says.

Harris had mellowed and become more philosophical about life. He liked to reflect, 'In life you have to run the length of your own wildness, testing and examining every foot of the way.'

Once, when asked if he drank to ease the pain of his life, he said frankly, 'I drank because I enjoyed it. They tried to tell me I drank to escape but I said that if that were so, you'd spend the rest of your life escaping anyway. So I say to myself now, I am what I am now, and the reason I am what I am is of no interest to me whatsoever.'

To show that he did not object to others enjoying a drink, he ran up a bar bill of £1,000 in one night to celebrate the end of shooting of *The Field*. As the crew and cast made merry in the Renvyle House Hotel in the heart of Connemara, Harris sat sipping a cup of tea. Remarked Hugh Coyle, owner of the hotel, 'The first anybody knew about the big session was when a notice appeared on the hotel board. It read, "Drinks are on me for the night before exhaustion sets in – Richard Harris." '

He knew exactly when he gave up drink and where he stopped drinking. It was 11 August 1981 at 11.20 p.m. in the Jockey Club in Washington. As he recalled, 'I had the discipline to stop. Just like that. I had been collapsing in the street and on stage. I passed out at dinner one night and a doctor friend warned me it wasn't the booze. I had been in a coma: the alcohol was shooting too much insulin into the system. So I sat in the Jockey Club with a friend and said, "This is my last drink." I took the wine list and there were two bottles of Château Margaux 1957 at 325 dollars a bottle. I drank them both, and that was it.'

Nevertheless, if he had to live his life all over again, he said he wouldn't change it. He would marry the same two women, have the same children, live the same life. The only mistake he reckoned he made was that he stayed away from the theatre too long. Elizabeth was his best friend now. So were his sons.

In conversation, he tended to mention Elizabeth a lot, as though clinging to memories. Not so long ago he asked her what it was like to be married to him. She looked at him and replied, 'It was magic – until you had that one drink too many and then a veil dropped over your face.'

At the end of their marriage, he suspected the truth. 'Liz couldn't look at me. She could no longer live with that one too many. Now, looking back, I understand it totally.'

He could say he achieved most if not all of his ambitions as the 1990s approached. He no longer needed alcohol to excite him, to make life bearable, to escape from it all. Friends noticed his easy approach to living; he revelled in good conversation, good fellowship and good humour.

In Limerick, whatever his achievements, he would always remain Dickie Harris.

Filmography

1958 (début) *Alive and Kicking* (Associated British Films) with Sybil Thorndike, Kathleen Harrison, Estelle Winwood, Richard Harris. Director: Cyril Frankel.

1959 *Shake Hands with the Devil* (Troy Films) with James Cagney, Don Murray, Dana Wynter, Cyril Cusack, Michael Redgrave, Richard Harris. Director: Michael Anderson.

1959 *The Wreck of the Mary Deare* (A Blaustein–Baroda Production) with Gary Cooper, Richard Harris. Director: Michael Anderson.

1960 *A Terrible Beauty* (Raymond Stross DMR Productions) with Robert Mitchum, Anna Heywood, Dan O'Herlihy, Cyril Cusack, Richard Harris, Niall MacGinniss. Director: Tay Garnett.

1961 *The Long and the Short and the Tall* (Michael Balcon Productions) with Laurence Harvey, Richard Todd, Richard Harris, Ronnie Fraser. Director: Leslie Norman.

1961 *The Guns of Navarone* (Open Road) with Gregory Peck, Anthony Quinn, Stanley Baker, Anthony Quayle, Richard Harris, Irene Papas, Gia Scala. Director: J. Lee Thompson.

1962 *Mutiny on the Bounty* (MGM/Arcola) with Marlon Brando, Richard Harris, Trevor Howard, Hugh Griffith, Tarita, Richard Haydn, Noel Purcell. Director: Lewis Milestone.

1963 *This Sporting Life* (Rank Films) with Richard Harris, Rachel Roberts, Colin Blakely, Alan Badel, Arthur Lowe. Director: Lindsay Anderson.

1964 *The Red Desert* (Federiz Film/Duomile Francoriz Production) with Richard Harris, Monica Vitti. Director: Michelangelo Antonioni.

1965 *Major Dundee* (Columbia) with Charlton Heston, Richard Harris, James Coburn. Director: Sam Peckinpah.

1965 *Three Faces of a Woman* (A Dino de Laurentiis Production) with Richard Harris, Princess Soraya, Alberto Sordi. Directors: Antonioni, Mauro Bolognini and Franco Indovine.

1966 *Hawaii* (Mirisch Corporation) with Richard Harris, Julie Andrews, Max von Sydow. Director: George Roy Hill.

1966 *The Bible* (A Dino de Laurentiis Production) with Michael Parks, Ulla Bergryd, Ava Gardner, Peter O'Toole, Richard Harris, George C. Scott, Stephen Boyd. Director: John Huston.

1966 *The Heroes of Telemark* (Rank) with Kirk Douglas, Richard Harris, Ulla Jacobson, Michael Redgrave. Director: Anthony Mann.

1967 *Caprice* (20th Century Fox) with Doris Day, Richard Harris, Ray Walston, Jack Kruschen, Michael J. Pollard. Director: Frank Tashlin.

1967 *Camelot* (Warner Brothers) with Richard Harris, Vanessa Redgrave, Franco Nero, David Hemmings, Lionel Jeffries. Director: Joshua Logan.

1969 *The Molly Maguires* (Columbia) with Richard Harris, Sean Connery, Samantha Eggar, Frank Finlay. Director: Martin Fitt.

1970 *Cromwell* (Columbia) with Richard Harris, Alec Guinness, Robert Morley. Director: Ken Hughes.

1970 *Bloomfield* (World Film Services/Wolf Mankowitz & John Heyman in association with Limbridge Productions) with Richard Harris, Romy Schneider, Kim Burfield. Director: Richard Harris (his début).

1971 *Man in the Wilderness* (Warner Brothers) with Richard Harris, Prunella Ransome, John Huston, Ben Carruthers, Henry Wilcoxon. Director: Richard C. Sarafian.

1972 *A Man Called Horse* (Cinema Center/Sanford Howard Productions, USA) with Richard Harris, Corinna Topsei, Manu Toupu, Judith Anderson, Jean Gascon. Director: Elliot Silverstein.

1973 *The Deadly Trackers* (Cine Film Productions) with Richard Harris, Rod Taylor, Neville Brand. Director: Barry Sheer.

1974 *99 44/100 Dead* (Joe Wizan Vashon) with Richard Harris, Edmund O'Brien, Ann Turkel. Director: John Frankenheim.

1974 *Juggernaut* (United Artists) with Richard Harris, Omar Sharif, David Hemmings, Roy Kinnear, Cyril Cusack, Freddie Jones. Director: Richard Lester.

1975 *Echoes of Summer* (A Castle Service Company feature in association with Astral Bellevue PatheBryanston Dist., Inc.) with Richard Harris, Geraldine Fitzgerald, Lois Nettleton, Jodie Foster. Director: Don Taylor.

1976 *Robin and Marian* (Columbia) with Sean Connery, Audrey Hepburn, Robert Shaw, Richard Harris, Nicol Williamson, Denholm Elliot, Kenneth Haigh. Director: Richard Lester.

1976 *Return of a Man Called Horse* (United Artists) with Richard Harris, Gale Sondergaard, Geoffrey Lewis, Claudio Brook, Enrique Lucero. Director: Irwin Kershner.

1977 *The Cassandra Crossing* (Associated General Films (London)/Campagnia Cinematografica Champion (Rome) for International Cine Productions) with Richard Harris, Sophia Loren, Martin Sheen, Ava Gardner, Burt Lancaster. Director: George Pan Cosmatos.

1977 *Gulliver's Travels* (A Valeness–Belvision Production) with Richard Harris, Catherine Schell, Norman Shelley, Meredith Edwards, Director: Peter Hunt.

1977 *Orca – Killer Whale* (Dino de Laurentiis for Famous Films) with Richard Harris, Charlotte Rampling, Will Sampson, Keenan Wynn. Director: Michael Anderson.

1977 *Golden Rendezvous* (Film Trust–Milton Okun Productions/ Golden Rendezvous Productions) with Richard Harris, Ann Turkel, David Janssen, Burgess Meredith, John Vernon, Gordon Jackson. Director: Ashley Lazarus.

1978 *The Wild Geese* (Richard Films Productions/Rank) with Richard Burton, Richard Harris, Roger Moore, Hardy Kruger, Stewart Granger. Director: Andrew V. McLaglen.

1979 *Ravengers* (Cinecorps Productions/Columbia) with Richard Harris, Ernest Borgnine, Ann Turkel, Anthony James, Art Carney. Director: Richard Compton.

1979 *Game for Vultures* (Pyramid Pictures) with Richard Harris, Richard Roundtree, Joan Collins, Ray Milland. Director: James Fargo.

1981 *Tarzan, the Apeman* (Svengali for MGM) with Richard Harris, Bo Derek. Director: John Derek.

1985 *Martin's Day* (United Artists/World Film Services) with Richard Harris, Justin Henry, Lindsay Wagner, James Coburn, Karen Black, John Ireland. Director: Alan Gibson.

1989 *The Field* (Ferndale Films) with Richard Harris, Tom Berenger, John Hurt, Frances Tomelty, Brenda Fricker. Director: Jim Sheridan.

Index